...ships

s,

...ers

KoganPage

LONDON PHILADELPHIA NEW DELHI

First published in Great Britain and the United States in 2012 by Kogan Page Limited

120 Pentonville Road	1518 Walnut Street, Suite 1100	4737/23 Ansari Road
London N1 9JN	Philadelphia PA 19102	Daryaganj
United Kingdom	USA	New Delhi 110002
www.koganpage.com		India

© Catherine Dawson, 2012

The right of Catherine Dawson to be identified as the author of this work has been asserted by her in accordance with the Copyright, Designs and Patents Act 1988.

ISBN   978 0 7494 6333 5
E-ISBN   978 0 7494 6334 2

British Library Cataloguing-in-Publication Data

A CIP record for this book is available from the British Library.

Library of Congress Cataloging-in-Publication Data

Dawson, Catherine.
    Apprenticeships : for students, parents and job seekers / Catherine Dawson.
       p. cm.
    Includes bibliographical references and index.
    ISBN 978-0-7494-6333-5 – ISBN 978-0-7494-6334-2 (ebook)   1. Apprentices–Great Britain.
2. Occupational training–Great Britain.   3. Job hunting–Great Britain.
4. Career changes–Great Britain.   I. Title.
    HD4885.G7D39 2012
    331.702–dc23

Typeset by Graphicraft Ltd, Hong Kong
Print production managed by Jellyfish
Printed and bound in the UK by CPI Group (UK) Ltd, Croydon, CR0 4YY

Contents

Introduction

Apprenticeships provide the opportunity for employees (and trainees) to learn on the job, while receiving a wage. They have been available in various forms for hundreds of years in the UK and today are being promoted heavily as a legitimate and viable route into employment for young people and adults alike. Indeed, on 7 February 2011 Vince Cable, the Business Secretary, promised the creation of 100,000 new apprenticeships by 2014, with 75,000 of these being for adult apprentices.

This book has been written to provide comprehensive, down-to-earth information and advice for people wishing to know more about the modern-day apprenticeship scheme. It includes information about the history, background and type of apprenticeships available, along with practical information about finding, choosing and applying for an apprenticeship. It also contains advice on funding an apprenticeship, employment/training contracts, health and safety, mentoring and training, insurance issues, employment rights, redundancy and dismissal.

The book is aimed at the following groups of people:

- school pupils who are thinking about what to do after school;
- school and college leavers who need to make decisions about their future employment;
- school and college leavers who prefer to train on the job and receive a wage, rather than go to university;
- parents who want to find out more about modern-day apprenticeships to ascertain whether undertaking an apprenticeship would be a suitable route for their child;
- undergraduates who are thinking about future careers;
- graduates who have been unable to find a job, and who feel that they need to try an alternative route into employment;
- adults who are thinking about retraining or changing careers;
- people currently out of paid work who want to find employment through becoming an apprentice;
- full-time and part-time adult learners.

The book is divided into four sections. The first provides a general overview of the apprenticeship scheme, including the history, background, facts and figures, how it works, the types of apprenticeship that are available and information about the organizations that take part in, and run, the scheme.

The second section provides information for school, college and university students and adult learners. It helps them to weigh up the pros and cons, assess alternatives, choose the right scheme, make an application and complete the apprenticeship successfully.

The third section is aimed at parents. It provides information for those who want to know more about apprenticeships, those who are unsure about what an apprenticeship entails and parents who have misconceptions about the scheme. It provides information about how the scheme works and how it can be of benefit to young people. It also advises parents on how they can help with decision making and offer support before, during and after their child's apprenticeship programme.

The fourth section is aimed at jobseekers, including people who are out of work and those who are looking to change their careers. Often adults are overlooked when apprenticeships are described. However, apprenticeships are available for adults, despite government funding being directed heavily towards younger groups. Adults, therefore, are now viewing apprenticeships as a useful way to change, or progress in, their chosen career. Also, the opportunities for adults are likely to increase as more funding becomes available for the adult apprenticeship scheme.

Appendix 1 lists the types of apprenticeship that are available in each sector and contains examples of the job roles that are available for Level 2, Level 3 and Level 4 apprenticeships, where applicable. Appendix 2 asks and answers some common questions about apprenticeships. Appendix 3 goes on to provide two detailed case studies from apprentices, illustrating how they found out about their apprenticeship and highlighting some of the good and bad points they have encountered. (Please note that quotations in Appendix 3 and throughout the book have been edited slightly to enhance readability.) Appendices 4 and 5 go on to provide useful addresses and websites for anyone who wishes to follow up any of the information provided in the book.

I have worked in the education sector for almost 30 years, teaching adults and conducting research with young people, students, jobseekers, apprentices and employers. My research has highlighted the importance of providing practical, down-to-earth information about learning and earning opportunities so that people can make informed choices based on sound information and practical examples.

Apprenticeships can and do provide an opportunity for people to begin and progress within their chosen career. However, if you intend to follow this route it is important that you make the right choices and receive the best possible information, advice and guidance. Through doing this you will be able to avoid problems that can occur during your apprenticeship and overcome pitfalls that may arise as a result of making inappropriate choices.

This book provides detailed information and advice that will help you to make the right decisions. It will also help you to deal with (and overcome) problems if and when they occur. I hope that you find this book useful and I wish you every success with your apprenticeship and chosen career.

Part One
Knowing about apprenticeships

Chapter One
The development of apprenticeships

Today apprenticeships are nationally recognized programmes designed by industry to equip young people and adults with practical skills for work. However, apprenticeships, in various forms, have been utilized for centuries as a means of passing on skills and trades from a 'master' to an apprentice ('master' could include both men and women, for example seamstresses took on apprentices). Indeed, early on in the development of apprenticeships it was illegal for someone to learn a craft without having paid the required fee to the authorities to become an official apprentice.

Rules and regulations have changed constantly over the centuries, usually in response to technological and political changes, eventually metamorphosing into the system that we see today. This chapter gives a brief history of apprenticeships and discusses the structure and framework of the current apprenticeship system.

History and background

The first official use of the term 'apprentice' was during the Middle Ages. Prior to this time workers had passed on their skills and knowledge to their own children and to local younger workers on an informal basis, without a specific system in place. However, as this system was based on private contract between apprentice and master it could be open to abuse by either party. Therefore, during the 14th and 15th centuries it was felt that some type of regulation was required to bring order to the system. For example, new regulations were introduced that meant that masters could no longer force their apprentices to carry out tasks outside their trade and apprentices were expected to be 'obedient, industrious and orderly' (Thomas, 1929).

In the Middle Ages apprentices tended to be aged 10 to 15 years. They would provide cheap labour in exchange for food, lodgings, necessary woollen and linen clothing, and training in a trade or craft. They had to agree to train for a minimum of seven years, after which they could progress to the positions of craftsman, journeyman, master and eventually grandmaster. Many apprentices, however, served for a much longer period and in some cases were almost 'adopted' by their masters (Thomas, 1929). This was often the case when masters would receive boys only from their own village or town.

> Despite being self-employed, Belper nailers founded a kind of trade union with rules setting out conditions whereby young boys could enter the trade. So tight were the rules that only the children of established nailers could normally learn to be a nailer, an occupation he could only claim after seven years of apprenticeship. Despite being unionized, nailers were forbidden to buy stock rods from anywhere other than from approved nailmasters or factors, otherwise they faced a heavy fine. Anyone attempting to take on an apprentice from outside the closely linked family network could only do so by paying a premium of £20 to the union, a massive sum to a working class man in the 19th century.
>
> Spencer, B (2011) 'Belper Nailers',
> *Country Images*, March 2011, pp 34–35

In 1802 the Health and Morals of Apprentices Act was passed. Under this Act, new regulations covering working conditions and training for apprentices were introduced. This included the introduction of a 12-hour working day and the requirement that factory apprentices were taught reading, writing and arithmetic. It also instructed that male and female apprentices were to be provided with separate sleeping accommodation and that there should not be more than two apprentices to sleep in one bed. The Statute of Artificers and Apprentices, which had been introduced in 1563, had forbidden anyone from practising a trade or craft without first serving a seven-year period as an apprentice. However, this was repealed in 1814 so that practising a skill without being an apprentice was no longer illegal (National Apprenticeship Service, 2011).

CASE STUDY

I found details of my dad's apprenticeship where he had dispensation in 1915 to leave school at 13 and start his engineering apprenticeship at a local firm. He stayed with the firm all his working life, ending up as the chief engineer for the factory. He again did what interested him, his hobby being a model engineer. So I had several nice working toys. The idea of being able to leave school early means you can learn what you need to learn as an apprentice without being bothered with all the other useless subjects being forced on you.

SOURCE Boots, Portland, apprentice 1955–60, via e-mail

As the 19th century progressed apprenticeships were expanded to include the emerging industries of engineering and shipbuilding, with plumbing, car mechanics and electrical apprenticeships introduced as technology progressed in the 20th century. Despite these new industries, apprentice numbers declined in the 1960s and 1970s. This was due, in part, to the increasing opportunities available in full-time education and the growing number of training schemes for young people (National Apprenticeship Service, 2011). Also, apprenticeships were criticized for providing limited opportunities for women and for not including many of the newer occupations that were emerging as the 20th century progressed.

CASE STUDY

Up to now we apprentices had a fairly easy time, as long as we were in the factory between 8 and 5 and looked as though we were doing something, we were pretty much left to our own devices... When Wellworthy took over, things changed dramatically. They sold the sports field which meant that my summer afternoons spent mowing it with the tractor and three-gang mower were at an end (in fact the tractor went too!). And we were all given specific responsibilities for part of the piston production line which they set up almost immediately. At 18 years old I had charge of part of a product line boring one-inch holes in pistons 'manned' by six women who were all about twice my age... I was very young and inexperienced for my age.

From the time that I had been taken on as an apprentice, I had been given 'day release' to attend Bridgwater Technical College provided that I did at least one evening per week at night school and Wellworthy carried this on, which enabled me to get a City and Guilds Diploma in machine shop engineering by the time I was 21 and left the factory.

SOURCE Ian Brooke, Weymouth, apprentice 1958–63, via e-mail

Modern apprenticeships

In 1993 John Major's government proposed the introduction of modern apprenticeships, which did not require pure technical training as they had done in the past, but instead focused on occupational competence (the skills and attributes required to carry out a specific job). This new apprenticeship system became functional in 1995 and has been revamped and reformed ever since.

In 2004 in England the then Secretary of State for Education and Skills, Charles Clarke, announced a series of reforms that included the introduction of young apprenticeships for 14–16-year-olds, making apprenticeships available to people aged over 25 and renaming foundation modern apprenticeships and advanced modern apprenticeships as 'apprenticeships' and 'advanced apprenticeships' respectively (see Chapter 2). Apprenticeships in Northern Ireland, Wales and Scotland have also been revamped and rebranded, although the title of 'modern apprenticeship' has been retained in Scotland.

The National Apprenticeship Service (NAS) was launched officially in April 2009. It was created to bring about 'a significant growth' in the number of employers offering apprenticeships. In June 2010 it was announced by Vince Cable that the Coalition government had plans to create 50,000 additional apprenticeships and that these were to be targeted particularly at places within small and medium businesses. A further announcement during National Apprenticeship Week in February 2011 promised the creation of 100,000 new apprenticeships by 2014, with 75,000 of these being for adult apprentices. The government believes that this increase in numbers will be good for young people, business and the economy. An important area of expansion includes plans for the government to co-fund 1,000 apprenticeship places in the nuclear energy sector and a further 2,500 apprenticeships in advanced wind energy.

Facts and figures

By the 16th century it is estimated that around 10 per cent of the population of London were apprentices (Thomas, 1929). Numbers continued to rise with more favourable legislation and as new trades emerged and developed. However, the 20th century saw a gradual decline of apprenticeships resulting in apprentice numbers reaching their lowest point in the 1970s.

It was not until the mid-1990s that a new surge in apprenticeships occurred, with the then Conservative government providing finance and incentives to encourage employers to become involved in the new apprenticeship scheme. In 1997 there were 75,000 apprentices. Today, according to the NAS, this has risen to 180,000 apprenticeships and, by the end of 2011, more than 900,000 learners are expected to have completed a full apprenticeship.

In September 2010 the Department for Education reported that there were over 130,000 employers offering apprenticeships and over 190 different types of apprenticeship available across 80 industry sectors. In 2010 the apprenticeship budget was £1,178 million (£780 million for 16- to 18-year-olds). The Department of Education reports that people with a Level 2 apprenticeship earn on average around £73,000 more over their lifetime than those with a Level 1 qualification or below; and people with an advanced apprenticeship earn around £105,000 more.

By 2014–15, John Hayes, the Skills Minister, hopes that that 400,000 people will be enrolled on apprenticeships, with half of them aged over 19 and funded by the Department for Business, Information and Skills. (Apprentices aged between 16 and 18 have their college training paid for by the Department for Education: see Chapter 2.)

The role of Sector Skills Councils

In 2001 the government announced its intention to replace National Training Organizations (which had previously determined the qualifications that made up apprenticeship frameworks in their skill area) with Sector Skills Councils (SSCs). In April 2009 there were 25 SSCs (often referred to as the 'network' of SSCs), the first of which was licensed in April 2003 and the remainder on a rolling programme until the final SSC received its licence in January 2006. In 2011, there are 23 SSCs following the closure of Skillfast-UK and the withdrawal of Government Skills from the SSC network. The objectives of the SSCs are fourfold:

- to reduce skills gaps and shortages;
- to improve productivity, business and public service performance;
- to increase opportunities to boost the skills and productivity of everyone in the sector's workforce, including action on equal opportunities;
- to improve learning supply, including apprenticeships, higher education and national occupational standards.

Approximately 90 per cent of the UK workforce falls into the remit of SSCs according to the Alliance of Sector Skills Councils (**www.sscalliance.org**). The 23 sectors are:

- property, facilities management, housing and cleaning;
- chemical and pharmaceutical, oil, gas, nuclear, petroleum and polymers;
- construction;
- craft, cultural heritage, design, literature, music, performing and visual arts;
- business and information technology, including software, internet and web, IT services, telecommunications and business change;
- gas, power, waste management and water industries;
- financial services, accountancy and finance;
- passenger transport;
- retail motor industries;
- food and drinks manufacturing and processing;
- environment and land-based;
- community learning, education, further education (FE), higher education (HE), libraries, work-based learning and training providers;
- hospitality, leisure, travel and tourism;
- building products, coatings, extractive and mineral processing, furniture, furnishings and interiors, glass and related industries, glazed ceramics, paper and printing and wood industry;
- science, engineering and manufacturing technologies;
- sport and recreation, health and fitness, outdoors, playwork and caravanning industry;
- social care, children, early years and young people's workforces in the UK;
- TV, film, radio, interactive media, animation, computer games, facilities, photo imaging and publishing;
- UK health;
- policing and law enforcement, youth justice, custodial care, community justice, courts service, prosecution services and forensic science;

- freight logistics and wholesaling industry;
- retail;
- building services engineering.

Contact details for each SSC are provided in Appendix 4. You can contact the relevant SSC direct to find out more information about the types of apprenticeships, jobs and careers that are available within each of the sectors described above. Alternatively, you can obtain more information about all the SSCs by visiting the Alliance of Sector Skills Councils website: **www.sscalliance.org**.

Frameworks

At this present time, apprenticeships are based on frameworks that are devised mainly by SSCs (other bodies can devise frameworks and the government is keen to encourage more organizations to get involved – see the Wolf Review, below). In 2011 there are 190 frameworks covering a wide variety of occupations. Each framework contains a number of elements that can be certified separately:

- A knowledge-based element such as a Technical Certificate, BTEC or City & Guilds qualification. This qualification equips the apprentice with the knowledge and understanding that underpins the NVQ competencies. The qualification tends to be completed away from the workplace, usually at an FE college, and offers a structured approach to teaching, including external assessment.

- A competence-based element such as a National Vocational Qualification (NVQ) or Scottish Vocational Qualification (SVQ). These qualifications assess competence and are designed around the skills people use at work. The apprenticeship programme provides apprentices with an NVQ at either Level 2 or Level 3.

- A Functional Skills element. This includes practical skills in English, information and communication technology and mathematics. This element replaced Key Skills in September 2010. Assessment requires apprentices to show that they can use skills confidently in a range of different situations (depending on the qualification level). They are expected to apply their skills in practical tasks and scenarios and to show that they can use problem-solving techniques effectively.

- Personal learning and thinking skills. All frameworks must clearly specify how the achievement of these elements is to be evidenced by the apprentice. Examples of this may be through completion of a specific qualification or through completion of a workbook. Six areas are to be covered:
  - independent enquiry;
  - creative thinking;
  - reflective learning;
  - team working;
  - self-management;
  - effective participation.
- Employer Rights and Responsibilities (ERR). This element includes issues such as rights and responsibilities of workers (including equal opportunities legislation), organization, disciplines and representative structures of the industries and the impact on the sector of public law and policies.

The role of Apprenticeship Training Agencies

An Apprenticeship Training Agency (ATA) is a not-for-profit organization that directly employs and manages individuals who undertake their apprenticeship with an approved training provider while being hired out to a 'host employer'. The host employer pays the ATA a fee for the hire of the apprentice. This fee is made up of their salary plus a service charge that covers the management costs of employing and supporting the apprentice. Administration dealing with issues such as payroll, support and supervision is carried out by the ATA (the legal employer of the apprentice). The government made available £7 million over two years from 2009/10–2010/11 to support approximately 10 to 15 pilot projects, to encourage expansion in ATAs and Group Training Associations (see below for more information about Group Training Associations).

Advantages

ATAs are popular amongst employers because the administrative load is reduced and they can request that the apprentice is sent back to the ATA with only two weeks' notice. The apprentice is able to move on to other hosts, which, supporters believe, widens opportunity and lessons risk for both employer and apprentice. The NAS believes that ATAs offer opportunity for apprentices 'to experience a range of employers and increased security around the continuation of their apprenticeship'.

Disadvantages

Trade unions have identified the following problems with the ATA system:

- The ATAs cannot give permanent job guarantees on completion of the apprenticeship.
- Host companies could use a succession of ATA trainees as a means of substituting for permanent jobs.
- Apprentices can be passed around a variety of employers without any wishing to commit to the whole apprenticeship course.
- ATAs make it difficult for unions to recruit and organize, which means that apprentices miss out on the benefits to be gained from union membership.
- Apprentices find it difficult to build up a lasting relationship with one employer, which means that they miss out on the benefits that can come from this type of relationship, such as a sense of company loyalty, promotion within the company and lasting friendships.

Contacting your regional ATA

At the present time there are 14 ATAs and these are listed in Table 1.1. Visit the website of the ATA in your region for more information (click on 'apprenticeships', where relevant, to be directed to the right pages).

CASE STUDY

On 22 September 2010 Leicester College held a breakfast launch event to celebrate its new apprenticeship service, the Apprenticeship Training Agency. The College was awarded funding to deliver public sector apprenticeships via this service in February 2010 and the service has been expanded recently to offer the new-style delivery of apprentices in the private sector. The breakfast event provided local employers with an opportunity to find out more about the service. For more information, visit **www.leicestercollege.ac.uk**.

TABLE 1.1 Apprenticeship Training Agencies in the UK

Region	ATA	Website
East of England	Essex Works	www.essex.gov.uk
East Midlands	Leicester College	www.leicestercollege.ac.uk
East Midlands	Vision Apprenticeships	www.wnc.ac.uk
London	SLB Logistics	www.southlondonbusiness.co.uk
London	Apprenticeship First	www.apprenticeshipsfirst.com
London	London Apprenticeship Company	www.londonapprenticeship.co.uk
National	Creative and Cultural NSA	http://nsa-ccskills.co.uk
North East	North East Apprenticeship Company	www.neapprenticeship.co.uk
North West	North West Apprenticeship Company	www.nwapprenticeship.co.uk
South East	South East Apprenticeship Company	www.se-apprenticeship.co.uk
South West	South West Apprenticeship Company	www.theswac.org.uk
West Midlands	Logistics Apprenticeship Training Academy	http://lataacademy.com
West Midlands	The Apprenticeship Works	www.theapprenticeshipworks.com
Yorkshire and Humber	Yorkshire and the Humber Apprenticeship Training Agency	www.yhata.org

The role of Group Training Associations

A Group Training Association (GTA) is a non-profit organization providing training and related services on behalf of a group of local employers. Some are funded by the Skills Funding Agency or Young People's Learning Agency (these organizations replaced the Learning and Skills Council in March 2010), whereas others are financed and controlled by local companies.

GTAs were originally set up in the 1960s to undertake training for groups of subscribing employers. This included advising on workforce development, analysing training needs, and providing health and safety training and management training. In terms of apprenticeships, the GTAs' curriculum was centred initially on apprenticeships for engineering, construction and manufacturing. Today, however, their work has expanded to cover a wide variety of sectors, including:

- engineering (including mechanical, electrical, design, fabrication/welding);
- business and administration;
- information technology;
- customer service;
- accountancy;
- warehouse and distribution.

GTAs have evolved over the years and now offer training in technical and work skills for young apprenticeships in schools, and also provide graduate and adult apprenticeships. Today, GTAs are able to provide the following services:

- access to employment for apprentices;
- selection, recruitment and interviewing of apprentices for businesses;
- group and individual training;
- the development of personal, tailor-made training programmes for apprentices;
- guidance and support for employers and apprentices;
- information and help in applying for grants and funding for employers and apprentices;
- assessment and certification of qualifications;
- opportunities for qualification and career progression;

- the organization of local, district and national awards for apprentices (see case study, below);
- an adult working environment for apprentices and trainees.

Contacting your local GTA

In 2009 an umbrella organization for GTAs in England was created, called GTA England. This organization aims to raise the profile of GTAs, seek funding and devise relevant standards. For more information about GTA England visit **www.gta-england.com**. You can use the members' directory on this site to find contact details of your local GTA. If you live in other parts of the UK, visit the relevant SSC website to find contact details of your local GTA (see Appendix 4).

CASE STUDY

The North Humberside Motor Trades Group Training Association caters for the training needs of over 70 dealerships in the area. Each year the GTA holds an awards ceremony at which all certificates gained during the previous year are presented. The leading trainee in each specialism is awarded a trophy that is presented at the annual dinner. The GTA is also able to nominate apprentices for the Institute of the Motor Industry's District Awards and the Institute's National Awards. For more information about this GTA, visit **www.motortradesgta.org**.

The Wolf review

In autumn 2010 Michael Gove, the Secretary of State for Education, commissioned Professor Alison Wolf of King's College London to carry out an independent review of vocational education. A key recommendation of the report was to evaluate the delivery, structure and content of apprenticeships to ensure they deliver the right skills for the workplace. In the government response to the review, published in May 2011, it was stated that there are not enough apprenticeships available for 16–18-year-olds and that there are not enough incentives for employers to become involved in the scheme. As a result, the government has announced its intention to:

- look at the experience of other countries to simplify apprenticeships, remove bureaucracy and make them easier for employers to offer (this includes a review of payments to employers and making the system of employer benefits and payments more transparent);

- consider whether and how apprenticeship frameworks for 16–18-year-olds should be adapted to reflect the importance for this age group of a broader programme of study, and come forward with proposals in autumn 2011;

- phase out Key Skills from apprenticeship frameworks by September 2012 (Functional Skills and GCSEs will be the only recognized pathways to achieving the compulsory English and maths elements of an apprenticeship);

- encourage other bodies to draw up apprenticeship frameworks and review the role of SSCs (see above);

- produce an action plan based on an evaluation of the work of GTAs and ATAs (see above) carried out by the NAS;

- look into ways to encourage smaller employers to offer apprenticeship places.

Summary

Apprenticeships, in various forms, have been utilized for centuries as a means of passing on skills and knowledge from one generation to the next. Today apprenticeships are nationally recognized programmes that offer young people and adults the opportunity to earn while they learn and gain qualifications in their chosen sector. Apprenticeships are based on frameworks that are devised by SSCs, covering areas such as technical competence and functional skills. GTAS and ATAs work with employers to select, recruit and train apprentices for the private and public sectors.

In the UK there are various levels of apprenticeship available, including introductory levels for school pupils or those with few qualifications, Level 2 and Level 3 apprenticeships and higher apprenticeships for people interested in study at foundation degree level. These different levels are discussed in the following chapter.

References

National Apprenticeship Service (2011) [accessed 10 January, 2011] *History of Apprenticeships*, [online] http://www.apprenticeships.org.uk/ About-Us/History-of-Apprenticeships.aspx

Thomas, AH (1929) [accessed: 11 February 2011] 'Introduction: Apprenticeship', *Calendar of the plea and memoranda rolls of the city of London: volume 2: 1364–1381* (1929), pp XXX–XLVII, [online] http://www.british-history.ac.uk/ report.aspx?compid=36671

Chapter Two
The different levels of apprenticeship

There are different levels of apprenticeship available, depending on your age, competence and where you live and wish to train in the UK. Some of these schemes are college-based and available for young people, whereas others are work-based and available for people of all ages. Apprenticeships are also available for people with disabilities. These schemes are described in this chapter.

Young Apprenticeships (England and Wales)

In 2011 the Young Apprenticeship scheme is a programme in England and Wales that offers the opportunity for young people aged 14–16 to take industry-specific vocational or vocationally related qualifications alongside their programme of GCSEs. On this programme school pupils study at school for their GCSEs and also take part in vocation training, usually over two days a week, at a local college or training provider. The programme takes two years to complete and on successful completion the apprentice will receive a Level 2 nationally recognized vocational or equivalent qualification. The scheme is government funded so there is no cost to apprentices or employers (the Welsh Assembly Government funds the scheme in Wales).

The scheme provides the opportunity to undertake up to 50 days' work experience during the programme. However, since this programme is considered to be part of a young person's education, there is no payment available for training or work experience, although travelling expenses will be reimbursed. In most cases apprentices are only expected to undertake work experience during school hours, although some occupations, such as health and social care, may require work experience at other times (see case study below). If this is the case, apprentices and parents will be told in advance so that they can decide whether to take part in the scheme.

From September 2010, 10,000 Young Apprenticeship places were available, although not all schools take part in this scheme. Therefore, if you are interested in becoming a young apprentice you need to contact your school or local Connexions service to find out whether the scheme is available. At the present time, government policy for vocational education is under review, and the Young Apprenticeship scheme will be considered (and may be revised) when policy is formulated.

CASE STUDY

Young Apprenticeships are offered in health and social care. Work placements cover the health care, social care and early years sectors in equal proportion, which usually equates to 17 days in each sector. All placements are health and safety checked and a full risk assessment completed to cover the types of activities that are undertaken by the apprentice. Young people will not be placed in high-risk environments where the risk outweighs the experience, which includes places such as accident and emergency departments, for example. For more information about Young Apprenticeships in health and social care, visit **www.yahealthandsocialcare.org.uk**.

Programme-Led Apprenticeships (Northern Ireland)

The Programme-Led Apprenticeship (PLA) scheme was introduced in response to the economic downturn, when thousands of young people were leaving school and were unable to obtain a paid apprenticeship. Although ministers in the Northern Ireland Assembly are keen to develop and refine the PLA scheme, the NAS decided not to fund any new PLAs in England after 6 April 2011. This scheme, therefore, is now only available in Northern Ireland.

Through this scheme young people are able to study parts of the apprenticeship framework at a local college or training provider, even if they have been unable to secure a work placement. Once a suitable employer is found, they can then move on to their work placement and on-the-job training. Trainees on this scheme are considered to be in education and training, so do not receive a wage for any work placements they undertake. However, trainees in Northern Ireland may be able to apply for the Education Maintenance Allowance (EMA), which currently stands at £30 a week (see further information below).

There have been many critics of the PLA scheme, including employers and apprentices themselves. Criticisms include the following points:

- Using the word 'apprenticeship' is misleading because it implies that young people will spend their time learning a trade from their employer. In reality they spend most of their time in college with only minimal work experience.

- Unscrupulous employers may be tempted to make paid apprentices redundant in order to take on a free apprentice from the PLA scheme.

- Young people on the scheme can't get a placement because employers are unwilling to take part in the scheme. For example, in Northern Ireland 50 per cent of participants on the scheme in 2009/10 did not have placements with local employers, according to Dolores Kelly (Social Democratic and Labour Party), Northern Ireland Assembly, 2010.

- A one-day-a-week placement, from the employer's perspective, does not provide meaningful work experience for apprentices.

- A one-day placement is insufficient to meet the criteria for the required vocational qualification (usually NVQ Level 2).

- The costs of insuring trainees for one day a week are too much for some employers.

Recent Northern Ireland Assembly debates have highlighted the need to revamp and improve the programme so that some of these problems can be addressed. At the time of writing it is unclear if and when changes to the scheme will be made.

Pathways to Apprenticeships (Wales)

The Pathways to Apprenticeships (PTA) scheme was introduced in Wales as a result of the economic downturn. This programme is similar to the PLA scheme described above. It provides the opportunity for young people aged between 16 and 25 to undertake an intensive course of training at an FE college so that they can achieve a Level 2 qualification and progress on to a full apprenticeship. The FE framework is set by the relevant SSC (see Chapter 1).

Work experience is included within the programme and participants receive a training allowance of £30 a week (non-means-tested) subject to satisfactory attendance and progress. Bonuses are also provided along with the tools and equipment needed for their chosen occupation, up to a value of £200. In 2010 there were 2,000 places available through this scheme.

CASE STUDY

Bridgend College, together with the Welsh Assembly and SEMTA, the SSC for Science, Engineering and Manufacturing Technologies, offers a PTA programme in Engineering. It is a one-year full-time programme for which trainees receive a training allowance of £30 a week, subject to satisfactory progress and attendance. One day per week is spent undertaking an appropriate further education (or technical) certificate in either mechanical or electrical engineering. Four days a week are spent on the 'Performing Engineering Operations' (PEO) Level 2 qualification and Key Skills/Functional Skills. The programme includes a minimum of five weeks' work experience, carried out during half-term and term breaks.

Entry requirements for this programme are five GCSEs at A* to C, including mathematics, English and science, an appropriate work-based learning pathway or the Foundation Welsh Baccalaureate. For more information about this programme, visit **www.bridgend.ac.uk/ pathwaystoapprenticeships**.

Pre-Apprenticeship Learning (Wales)

The Pre-Apprenticeship Learning (PAL) scheme is available for people of any age in Wales who are in employment. It enables them to develop their literacy and numeracy skills so that they can progress on to a full apprenticeship. Although there is no age limit to accessing this qualification, all learners need to be employed in the occupational area in which they are choosing to study.

Before taking part in the programme employees undergo an assessment to identify specific basic skills needs. On successful completion of the programme, a further basic skills assessment is completed to determine progression and improvement. The programme is delivered primarily on a one-to-one basis by qualified basic skills tutors. Employees should be able to move on to a full apprenticeship after they have successfully completed their course. The qualifications delivered within this programme include a Certificate in Numeracy Entry Levels 1–3 and a Certificate in Literacy Entry Levels 1–3. To find out more about this scheme in Wales contact the SSC that covers your occupational sector (see Appendix 4 for contact details and Chapter 1 for more information about SSCs).

Apprenticeships (England and Northern Ireland)

'Apprenticeship' is the term that is used for apprenticeships that are offered at Level 2 in England and Levels 2 and 3 in Northern Ireland (in some cases apprentices may be able to begin their training at Level 1 and work towards a Level 2 qualification once this has been achieved). In Wales the term 'foundation apprenticeship' is used for apprenticeships at Level 2 and the term 'apprenticeship' used for the scheme at Level 3 (see below).

Apprenticeships are available to anyone who has attained the minimum school leaving age. However, owing to the way apprenticeships are funded (see Chapter 3) they tend to be offered to three different age groups:

- 16–18 years;
- 19–24 years;
- 25 and over (Adult Apprenticeships).

Apprenticeships are made up of five parts:

- NVQ Level 2 (equivalent to 5 GCSE passes at A* – C).
- Functional Skills Level 1/2. These are practical skills in English, information and communication technology and mathematics that allow people to work confidently, effectively and independently in life. They replaced Key Skills in September 2010, although Key Skills qualifications will still be recognized within apprenticeship frameworks until September 2016.
- Technical Certificate at Level 2.
- Employer Rights and Responsibilities (ERR), including issues such as health and safety and equal opportunities.

- Personal learning and thinking skills (evidence of these must be demonstrated, perhaps through a workbook or attaining specific qualifications, for example).

These apprenticeships help to develop the skills necessary for apprentices to work within their chosen career, and provide the opportunity to move on to an Advanced Apprenticeship in England or a Level 3 apprenticeship in Northern Ireland.

CASE STUDY

In September 2010, the Clothworkers' Foundation provided £10,000 to enable two trainees to undertake the 12-month-long training that is required as part of the new Heritage Specialist Apprenticeship Programme in Stonemasonry that is being offered by Stone Federation GB.

Two bursaries of £5,000 each were paid to two employers to support a trainee throughout the delivery of the programme, which began in September 2010.

The funding was administered by ConstructionSkills (the SSC), but the selection process for this bursary was undertaken by the Natural Stone Industry Training Group (NSITG). Consideration for the bursary was given to applicants who did not have access to other sources of grant funding. For more information about the Clothworkers' Foundation, visit **www.clothworkers.co.uk**. For more information about ConstructionSkills, visit **www.cskills.org** and for more information about the NSITG and Stone Federation GB, visit **www.stone-federationgb.org.uk**.

Foundation Apprenticeships (Wales)

Foundation Apprenticeships (FAs) are offered in Wales and are similar to the apprenticeships described above. They are available for people who wish to undertake up to two years of on-the-job training to work towards an NVQ Level 2. They are available in many career areas such as caring, engineering, office work, construction work, sport and recreation. Apprentices are paid a wage for the job if they are with an employer or a training allowance if they are on placement at a training centre.

CASE STUDY

Acorn is a training provider that offers a Foundation Apprenticeship in Retail Skills. The programme is suitable for people who are involved in retail as their primary work activity and wish to receive recognition for their retail skills and experience. It is also suitable for people who are new to a retail career and wish to work towards professional qualifications.

The apprenticeship consists of qualifications that are included in the Credit and Qualifications Framework for Wales (CQFW) and provides a flexible approach to learning through the selection of units and credits. The qualifications within the apprenticeship include a Level 2 Certificate in Retail Skills, a Level 2 Certificate in Retail Knowledge and Key Skills/Functional Skills qualifications at Level 1. For more information about this programme, visit **www.acorn-wales.co.uk/training**. For more information about the CQFW, visit **http://wales.gov.uk** (enter CQFW into the search box to be directed to the right pages).

Advanced Apprenticeships (England)

Advanced Apprenticeships are available in England for people who wish to work and train at Level 3. They are open to people over the age of 16 who have the necessary skills and qualifications (offered in the age bands described above). This usually means five GCSE passes at Grade C or above or the completion of an apprenticeship. In Scotland the term 'modern apprenticeship' is used for apprenticeships at Level 3 and above (see below) and in Wales the term 'apprenticeship' is used (see below). Advanced Apprenticeships are made up of various parts:

- a competence-based element: NVQ Level 3 (equivalent to 2 A levels);
- a knowledge-based element: Technical Certificate at Level 3;
- Functional Skills Level 2;
- Employer Rights and Responsibilities;
- personal learning and thinking skills;
- additional elements (depending on the sector and type of work).

Once an Advanced Apprenticeship has been completed, participants can move on to a Higher Apprenticeship, foundation degree or full-time employment.

CASE STUDY

Land Rover provide Advanced Apprenticeship programmes covering various motor dealership disciplines, including service technicians, body repair and paint refinishing. All Land Rover apprentice training is conducted in regular blocks at dedicated Land Rover training facilities by Land Rover instructors and assessors. Mentors look after apprentices during their work, and instructors and assessors pay regular visits to provide assistance and make sure that apprentices are developing on the programme.

In their final year apprentices are given the opportunity to take part in the Make a Difference (MAD) programme, which involves participation in a community project in the African bush, Amazon rainforest or Indian subcontinent. In 2010 the event was in its fifth year and is very popular among apprentices. For more information about the Land Rover apprenticeship programme, visit **www.landroverapprenticeships.com**.

Modern Apprenticeships (Scotland)

Modern Apprenticeships (MAs) in Scotland are available for people over the age of 16 who are capable of achieving a Scottish Vocational Qualification (SVQ) at Level 3 or above. SVQs are developed by SSCs, in partnership with industry and awarding bodies, and are based on a set of competencies that demonstrate a candidate's ability to work in real conditions. For more information about SVQs, visit the Scottish Qualifications Authority website: **www.sqa.org.uk**.

MAs can take between two and four years to complete (depending on level and competence) and are made up of three parts:

- SVQ Level 3 (in some cases candidates may be able to work towards a Level 2 qualification before moving on to a Level 3 qualification. Candidates may also have the opportunity to continue their training and work towards a Level 4 qualification).
- Core skills training, which includes:
  - communication;
  - working with others;
  - numeracy;
  - information technology;
  - problem solving.

- Additional components that vary from industry to industry, but may include additional units from other SVQs, industry-specific qualifications, or academic qualifications such as Higher National Certificates and Diplomas.

CASE STUDY

In 2011 the University of Glasgow offered Modern Apprenticeships in the following areas: administration, lab technicians, mechanical engineering, electrical engineering, IT professional and using IT. Entry requirements vary from sector to sector. As an example, administration apprentices should preferably have, or be working towards, Highers or Intermediate 2 in English and administration or business management. A good group of Standard grades in the relevant subjects will also be considered. For more information, visit **www.gla.ac.uk**.

Apprenticeships (Wales)

In Wales the term 'apprenticeship' is used to describe the scheme at Level 3. It is similar to the Advanced Apprenticeship scheme available in England and the Modern Apprenticeship scheme available in Scotland, described above. This scheme is available to people in Wales of any age and combines practical job training with off-the-job learning. Apprentices receive a wage, with employers contributing to training costs.

CASE STUDY

Tata Steel recruits approximately 50 apprentices a year in Port Talbot and Llanwern in areas such as manufacturing, engineering and business improvement. Benefits offered include a wage of up to £9,500 a year (2011), a company pension, the chance to obtain nationally recognized qualifications and free personal protective equipment, including overalls and safety footwear.

Applicants must have achieved or expect to achieve a minimum of three GCSE passes at Grade C or above, to include maths, English language and science. Applications are also invited from FE/HE students participating in engineering/science-based courses, ie National Certificate, GNVQ Science or relevant A levels as an alternative to GCSE Science. For more information about these apprenticeships, visit **www.tatasteeleurope.com/en/careers/**.

Higher Apprenticeships (England)

Higher Apprenticeships are available in England for people who wish to train and work towards a Level 4 qualification or a knowledge-based qualification such as a foundation degree. They are open to people who have the necessary skills and qualifications, which usually means A levels (or equivalent) or the successful completion of an Advanced Apprenticeship. Some employers may require candidates to take a literacy and numeracy test on application. Progression routes include full-time employment or study for an undergraduate degree.

CASE STUDY

Airbus offers a number of Higher Apprenticeships, including programmes in design, manufacturing support and product development. Training and academic study leads to a foundation degree in Aeronautical Engineering and NVQ Level 4 in Engineering Management. Entry requirements for these apprenticeships are six Bs at GCSE or equivalent including maths, English and science plus two Cs at A level (or equivalent) to include either maths or physics. For more information about Higher Apprenticeships at Airbus, visit **www.airbus.com/en/careers**.

Apprenticeships for people with disabilities

The Disability Discrimination Act (DDA) makes it unlawful for employers to discriminate on the grounds of disability. Also, all organizations that are involved in the development of apprenticeship frameworks are required to adhere to disability legislation. Despite this, people with disabilities and/or learning difficulties are still under-represented within apprenticeship programmes. The government, therefore, has set up a number of pilot schemes in an attempt to tackle these issues. For example, Triangle Training are undertaking a project funded by the Skills Funding Agency and the National Apprenticeship Service that aims to increase the number of apprenticeships taken up by 'atypical' apprentices, which includes people with learning difficulties. For more information about this scheme, visit **www.trianglefusion.co.uk**.

If you have a disability and are interested in an apprenticeship at any of the levels described above, contact Remploy for help and advice. This organization works with disabled people and employers to increase employment opportunities and to get rid of the barriers that prevent disabled people from working. Remploy has a dedicated Apprenticeship Team that will offer advice, support and access to funding for employers and apprentices. For more information, visit **www.remploy.co.uk**.

The Access to Work scheme was set up to help and support people with disabilities and employers by offering advice, practical support and financial assistance to help overcome work-related obstacles resulting from disability. Financial help for apprenticeships may be available through this scheme. For more information, visit **www.direct.gov.uk/accesstowork**.

Summary

There are various levels of apprenticeship available for people living in the UK who wish to become an apprentice. These programmes vary depending on age, competence and locality. Some schemes provide the opportunity for apprentices to move on to a higher level (with the same employer) on successful completion of their qualifications. Other progression routes include moving on to full-time study or full-time employment, either with the same employer or with a new employer. All levels of apprenticeship should be available for people with disabilities, although this group, at present, is under-represented in apprenticeship programmes.

Now that you understand more about the levels of apprenticeship scheme that are available, it is important to find out more about the practical aspects of apprenticeship programmes. This includes issues such as funding, working conditions, salaries and/or training allowance, assessment and contracts. These issues are discussed in the following chapter.

Further information

Apprenticeships: England

www.apprenticeships.org.uk
This is the website of the National Apprenticeship Service. On this site you can find out more about all types of apprenticeship in England and use the database to access information about specific apprenticeships.

Apprenticeships: Scotland

www.skillsdevelopmentscotland.co.uk

This is the website of Skills Development Scotland (SDS), which is Scotland's skills public body that operates across Scotland as a whole. On this site you can find out more about MAs and access some interesting case studies.

Apprenticeships: Northern Ireland

www.nidirect.gov.uk/apprenticeshipsni

This is the apprenticeship section of nidirect, which provides information about government services in Northern Ireland. These pages contain comprehensive information about apprenticeships in Northern Ireland for apprentices and employers. There are some interesting case studies and useful frequently asked questions to be found on this site.

Apprenticeships: Wales

http://wales.gov.uk

This is the website of the Welsh Assembly Government. Enter 'apprenticeships' into the search box to find information about the various schemes available in Wales, including the PTA scheme and the PAL scheme.

Education Maintenance Allowance

www.emascotland.com

This is the EMA Scotland website, which provides all the information you need to know about the EMA in Scotland. There is a section for administrators, current students and new students.

www.studentfinancewales.co.uk

This is the website of Student Finance Wales. Visit the EMA/ALG micro site to find more information about the EMA in Wales. (The ALG is an Assembly Learning Grant of up to £1,500, paid to students from low-income families who are aged 19 or over, whereas the EMA is a fortnightly allowance paid to students from low-income households aged 16–18.)

www.delni.gov.uk

This is the website of the Department for Employment and Learning in Northern Ireland. Enter 'EMA' into the search box to be directed to all the information you require about the EMA in Northern Ireland. Application forms and guidance notes can be downloaded from this site.

Chapter Three
How apprenticeships work

In the previous chapter we saw that there are various levels of apprentice-ship available, depending on age, where people live and their previous experience and qualifications. These levels also have an influence on the type of funding that is available (from government and from employers), the type of training that is received (employment or college-based) and the contract of employment, including salary and length of programme. These issues are discussed in this chapter.

Funding

Funding for apprenticeships in England is available from the National Apprenticeship Service (NAS). In Wales, similar funding is provided by the Welsh Assembly Government, in Scotland by the Scottish Government and in Northern Ireland by the Northern Ireland Government. In general, funding is paid directly to the organization that provides and supports the apprenticeship. For small and medium businesses, this funding, therefore, will go straight to the learning provider. Some large businesses, however, may have their own training centres that provide the apprenticeships and, if they have a direct contract with the NAS (or relevant government department), they will receive the funding themselves.

The amount of funding depends on the age of the apprentices and the sector in which the apprenticeship is offered. If apprentices are aged 16–18 years old, an organization/learning provider will receive 100 per cent of the cost of the training; if they are 19–24 years old, up to 50 per cent will be paid; if they are 25 years old or over, the organization/learning provider may only get a contribution depending on the sector and area in which it operates. (At the time of writing there are a small number of organizations that are now offering fully funded Adult Apprenticeships and it is hoped that this number will increase as more funding becomes available: see Chapter 15.)

This tiered funding system helps to explain why some apprenticeships are offered only to specific age groups. Age discrimination rules are complex where apprenticeships are concerned. This is because recent age discrimination legislation prohibits discrimination on the basis of age in employing apprentices, yet the funding of apprenticeships is exempt from this legislation (as funding from the government is targeted at young people below the age of 19). This means that both training providers and employers target apprenticeships at younger age groups that attract the most funding. However, if an employer advertises to a specific age group, without being able to demonstrate legitimate reasons to discriminate on the grounds of age, it is possible that they can be accused of age discrimination. More information about this issue is provided in Chapter 13. Also, see Laura's case study in Appendix 3 for an insight into the personal impact of these funding issues.

Funding is only available to cover the full cost of the mandatory training required to complete the framework as determined by the relevant SSC (see Chapter 1). If an employer decides to offer additional qualifications outside this framework, costs will have to be met by the employer or learning provider.

Although funding is available for training, employers are expected to meet the costs of wages, supervision, support and mentoring. However, the NAS points out that the costs of recruitment can be reduced if employers use the free online recruitment tool that matches apprentices with prospective employers (provided by the NAS for apprenticeships in England). Similar services are available in other parts of the UK.

Working with learning providers

Employers work with learning providers to make sure that the training meets the needs of the apprentice and the employer. Learning providers can be local FE colleges or specialist training organizations. If an employer decides that they wish to take on an apprentice they can choose a learning provider by contacting their local college or through using the service available on the NAS website in England (**www.apprenticeships.org.uk**). Similar services are available in other parts of the UK. Alternatively, employers may be approached by local learning providers who are seeking employers who can offer work placements for their apprentices (this may be the case for Programme-Led Apprenticeships, for example: see Chapter 2). Large employers in all parts of the UK may have their own training centres that provide day or block release training and assessment for apprentices.

When employers work with a local training provider they are allocated an employer representative who is able to:

- offer advice about apprenticeships and how they work;
- help to make choices about the most appropriate apprenticeship;
- provide information about available funding;
- discuss and agree a suitable training plan with the employer and apprentice;
- help with recruitment procedures;
- supervise/manage the training, ensuring that national standards are met;
- review the training, usually every 12 weeks;
- evaluate the training where necessary.

CASE STUDY

PGL Travel Ltd offers apprenticeships for activity instructors, water-sports instructors, chefs, hospitality staff and customer service staff. They take around a year to complete and comprise a mix of classroom-based learning that is undertaken over the winter when centres are not operational, combined with practical work, which is based on the job role. Benefits include a competitive wage, meals, free uniform and accommodation.

Successful applicants are required to undergo an enhanced Criminal Records Bureau (CRB) disclosure, which PGL will pay for. Applicants need to possess the legal right to live and work in the UK to be considered for these programmes. PGL is committed to the principle of equality and diversity and welcomes applicants from all sectors of the community. For more information about apprenticeships with PGL, visit **www.pgl.co.uk**.

Training and assessment

The Specification of Apprenticeship Standards for England (SASE) requires that an apprentice must receive at least 280 guided learning hours within the first year of their apprenticeship. (Following its introduction through the

Apprenticeships, Skills, Children and Learning Act 2009, the SASE was published by the Department for Business Innovation and Skills, Department for Education and the NAS on 20 January 2011.)

The type of learning/training offered to an apprentice depends on the type of apprenticeship, the sector, the size of employer and the training capabilities of employers and local training providers. Training takes place on the job and/or at a training centre or local college. Some apprentices may take part in training one day a week, for example, whereas others may undertake their training in blocks, perhaps for several weeks at a time. Apprentices on Programme-Led Apprenticeships and Young Apprenticeships undertake their training at school or college with some work placement incorporated into their course (see Chapter 2).

The learning provider appoints a training coordinator/assessor who works with the apprentice to ensure that the training is well planned and that there are no problems. Together with the apprentice and employer this person draws up an individual learning plan (also called a training and assessment plan) and a learning agreement. Some employers also decide to appoint a mentor at work (usually a more experienced employee working within the same sector as the apprentice). This person liaises with the training coordinator/assessor to make sure that the programme is meeting the needs of the apprentice and to check that the apprentice is progressing and meeting the required targets. See Table 3.1 for more information about the interaction and roles of employer, apprentice and training provider.

The training coordinator/assessor discusses the training and assessment of tasks in the workplace, establishing what type of evidence will be required to build a portfolio, and agrees suitable dates for observations and assessments in the workplace. These form part of the overall assessment plan. If an apprentice disagrees with an assessment decision that has been made by their assessor they have the right to appeal. (When an apprentice is taken on they are issued with an appeals procedure document from the awarding body.) If apprentices want to appeal they have to do so as soon as possible so that an internal verifier can adjudicate. The training coordinator/assessor completes an exit review to ensure that all components of the apprenticeship have been completed and to offer advice on possible progression opportunities.

TABLE 3.1 Roles of employer, apprentice and training provider

Employer	Apprentice	Training provider
Screen candidates to assess suitability for employment and interview if necessary	Apply for positions and attend all required interviews	Screen candidates to assess suitability for training and interview if necessary
Provide details of what the job entails and what will be expected of the apprentice	Understand and commit to work and training responsibilities	Explain training and qualification requirements to apprentice and employer
Agree on an individual learning plan for the apprentice	Agree to and sign an individual learning plan	Discuss and develop an individual learning plan with apprentice and employer
Read, commit to and sign learning agreement	Read, commit to and sign learning agreement	Produce and sign learning agreement, which identifies each partner's responsibility regarding training
Provide employment contract and information on health and safety, equality, diversity and grievance procedures, and ensure contract is not breached	Read and sign contract, and ensure contract is not breached	Carry out workplace inspection to check on issues such as health and safety and working conditions
Arrange appropriate insurance	Understand and commit to workplace rules and regulations	Check that appropriate insurance is in place
Assign a workplace mentor to offer guidance and support	Take responsibility for learning and work, build a good working relationship with mentor	Assign a dedicated training coordinator/assessor to the apprentice to manage the learning process
Carry out an induction to the workplace and introduce staff and other apprentices, where relevant	Attend all induction sessions when required	Carry out a formal induction to the college/training venue

TABLE 3.1 (*Cont'd*)

Employer	Apprentice	Training provider
Support and develop the apprentice through supervision and mentoring	Participate in regular reviews to gauge progress in training and work, attend all assessments/exams	Deliver required training and conduct regular reviews at least every 12 weeks
Pay a salary and other agreed benefits	Make all reasonable effort to achieve the relevant competencies and to develop as an employee	Support the apprentice throughout the programme and offer advice on progression routes

CASE STUDY

Barratt Development Plc has developed a Trade Apprenticeship Programme that combines college study with practical training over two years and leads to S/NVQ qualifications and a valuable trade. The programme begins in September each year. They have also developed a Technical Advanced Apprenticeship Programme, which is a new two-year scheme, designed for apprentices wishing to train in areas such as buying, design or surveying. This programme provides the opportunity to complete a number of 'on the job' modules, as well as an Ordinary National Certificate (ONC) or Higher National Certificate (HNC) at college. There is no set start date for this programme.

High fliers taking part in these programmes have the chance to join Barratt on a permanent basis and progress through the Barratt Academy. This includes another two years' study and training towards NVQ Level 3 and 4. At the end of year four, employees will have completed the Assistant Site Manager programme and will be ready to take the next step towards becoming a site manager or other roles across the Barratt Group. For more information about these programmes, visit **www.buildingcareerstogether.co.uk**.

Salaries

At the beginning of 2010 the National Minimum Wage (NWM) for an apprentice was £95 per week, although, on average, apprentices were paid £170 per week, according to the NAS. From October 2010 this was replaced by a NMW of £2.50 per hour for all apprentices aged under 19 and apprentices aged 19 or over in the first year of their apprenticeship (this will rise to £2.60 from October 2011). Employers can pay above this amount, if they wish. All apprentices over the age of 19 who have completed the first year of their apprenticeship are entitled to the NMW appropriate for their age (£6.08 for workers aged 21 and over and £4.98 for workers aged 18–20).

The NMW does not apply to apprenticeships that take place primarily at school or college, such as Young Apprenticeships or Programme-Led Apprenticeships, as apprentices are considered to be in full-time education (see Chapter 2). Instead, this type of apprenticeship attracts a training allowance or learners can apply for the Education Maintenance Allowance (EMA). For more information about the NMW and to find out current rates, visit **www.direct.gov.uk** and enter 'National Minimum Wage' into the search box to be directed to the relevant pages. For more information about the EMA, see Chapter 2. (The EMA has been withdrawn in England, but at the time of writing is still available in other parts of the UK.)

The following list provides an example of the types of salaries that apprentices are able to receive in the UK (2011 figures):

- Microsoft IT Support Apprentice based in Leeds: £100 per week;

- Business Administration/Customer Support Apprentice based in Altrincham: £95 per week for the first two months, £120 a week for the following two months and £150 a week for the remaining two months of the apprenticeship;

- Access Field Apprentice for Virgin Media, based in London: £12,000 per annum starting salary, rising to £18,350 on completion;

- Advanced Apprenticeships with the National Grid, nationwide: £13,000 per annum starting salary, rising to at least £18,000 on completion of the apprenticeship;

- Apprentice Brewer based in Aberdeenshire: £12,000–18,000 per annum, depending on qualifications and experience;

- Apprentice Technical Engineer for British Gas, nationwide: starting salary £5,000 per annum, rising to £19,400 on completion with the possibility of earning £30,000 as a qualified engineer.

Apprenticeship contracts

Apprentices have a special form of employment contract: in essence it is a contract for training, rather than for employment. An apprenticeship contract, therefore, is formed when an employer agrees to teach a trade and when an apprentice agrees to 'serve and learn'. Despite being a contract for training, apprenticeship programmes have been assimilated into employment law so that all employed apprentices are covered by the relevant employment legislation, in addition to the terms and conditions contained in their contract of employment.

The following contractual conditions apply to all apprentices who are employed for at least 16 hours a week. They do not apply to apprentices who are on Young Apprenticeship programmes, Programme-Led Apprenticeships or pre-apprenticeship learning programmes (see Chapter 2).

- Apprentices have the right to know the terms of employment. Apprentices who have worked for an employer for less than two months only have to have verbal terms. However, if apprentices have worked for an employer for more than two months they should receive a written statement or contract of employment. In practice, this is usually provided when an apprentice is offered their contract to sign.

- Apprentices must be offered work for a minimum of 16 hours a week, although most apprentices are employed full-time. (New legislation has come into force recently in England concerning apprenticeship working and training hours. The Apprenticeship 2010/11 Funding Requirements state that 'it is anticipated that all employed apprentices will be engaged in working and learning for a minimum of 30 hours per week' and the Apprenticeships, Skills, Children and Learning Act 2009 places a requirement on apprenticeship providers to ensure that all training takes place within contracted working hours.) Specific aspects of working hours, such as the actual hours of work and the number of breaks to be taken, are agreed by the employer and apprentice. All employees have the right under health and safety law to weekly and daily rest breaks. More information about health and safety at work can be obtained from **www.hse.gov.uk/workers** (England and Wales) and **www.safeandhealthyworking.com** (Scotland).

- Employers must give an adequate induction to the job and provide the necessary training (or time off for training) required to complete the apprenticeship. The contract should provide details relating to what training the apprentice will undertake and how this should be done (eg college, day release, attending different sites owned by the employer).

- Apprentices must be given at least 20 days' paid holiday per year as well as bank holidays.

- Apprentices are entitled to statutory Maternity Leave of 52 weeks with statutory Maternity Pay for up to 39 weeks.

- Employers must pay the wage that was advertised for the apprenticeship and this must be equivalent to, or more than, the NMW (see above). This includes time working plus the time spent on training both on and off the job, which also includes time at college.

- Apprentices have the right to a payslip that shows what has been paid and the deductions that have been made. This applies from the day that work starts. All apprentices over the age of 16 must pay tax and National Insurance on their income.

Express and implied contractual terms

All apprenticeship/employment contracts contain express terms (those that are explicitly agreed between apprentice and employer) and implied terms (those that are not specifically agreed between the employer and apprentice, but are based on custom, practice and agreement reached with trade unions and staff associations).

Express terms include those described above and, in most cases, will be listed in the employment contract, which apprentices will need to check and sign. However, express terms can also be included in other documents, such as job advertisements, staff manuals or handbooks and pay slips, or they can be made on a verbal basis. Therefore, all documentation (and a record of verbal agreements) should be kept by the apprentice in case there are any disputes at a later date.

Implied terms, in most cases, include the following points.

- Employer and apprentice have a duty of trust to each other. This means, for example, that an apprentice would not pass on company 'secrets' to competitors, or discuss their employer with competitors in a derogatory manner.

- Employer and apprentice have a duty of care to each other. The employer must provide a safe and healthy working environment and the apprentice must adhere to all health and safety rules and regulations.

- An apprentice has a duty to obey their employer, but only where 'reasonable'. Although the definition of 'reasonable' is not given, this is taken to mean that an employer should be obeyed when requests are within the law, within the remit of the employment contract and within health and safety guidelines.

- An employer has a duty to pay wages, even if there is no work available, unless the employment contract says otherwise.

Breaking a contract of employment

If either the employer or the apprentice does not follow a term in the contract, they can be considered to be 'in breach of contract'. Cases where this might occur include:

- An apprentice continually fails to turn up to work on a regular basis, without evidence that they are sick or have other recognized extenuating circumstances.

- An apprentice continually fails to attend the required training sessions, or carry out the work/study needed to obtain qualifications.

- An employer tries to make an apprentice redundant owing to the economic downturn (apprentices are protected against redundancy before their programme ends: see Chapter 16 for more information about redundancy and dismissal).

- An employer refuses to pay the stated salary.

- An employer orders an apprentice to carry out a task that is illegal (such as driving an untaxed vehicle).

An employer can try to dismiss an apprentice if they are in breach of contract and an apprentice can start grievance procedures against an employer if they are in breach of contract. However, both employer and apprentice should try to rectify all problems on an informal basis (and formal basis, if necessary) before instigating dismissal or grievance procedures. This is of particular importance for employers as they may find it very difficult to terminate the employment of an apprentice (see case study below). For more information about overcoming problems on an apprenticeship programme, see Chapters 8 and 16.

CASE STUDY

In 2006 an apprentice was awarded £24,000 for unfair dismissal after he was sacked before the end of his apprenticeship contract. The manufacturing firm based in Birmingham had dismissed the apprentice after three years owing to his alleged poor attendance record. However, a tribunal ruled that he had been wrongfully dismissed before his apprenticeship was completed and that his employer had not conducted his disciplinary hearing fairly. The apprentice was awarded £20,000 compensation for the breach of his apprenticeship contract, and £4,000 for unfair dismissal.

Apprenticeship Agreements

The Apprenticeships, Skills, Children and Learning Act 2009 refers to the introduction of an Apprenticeship Agreement in April 2011. However, at the time of writing the introduction of this Agreement has been delayed 'to allow more time for employers and training providers to prepare for its introduction and to ensure that the prescribed form which the Agreement must take is proportionate for business in terms of the cost implications' (NAS, March 2011).

Length of apprenticeship

The length of an apprenticeship depends on the type of programme and the capabilities of the apprentice. For example, Programme-Led Apprenticeships can run for up to one year, whereas apprenticeships at Level 2 can run for up to two years and Advanced Apprenticeships for up to three years. In some cases the Apprentice Agreement is instead designed specifically to allow the apprentice to gain a recognized qualification such as an NVQ Level 2, and does not state a specified time to achieve this qualification. If apprentices are able to achieve their qualifications within a shorter time-scale, and if their employment enables it, they can move on to the next level of apprenticeship.

Although apprenticeship contracts are for a fixed period of time (or until a specific qualification is achieved), they are not fixed-term contracts and are specifically excluded from the Fixed-Term Employees (Prevention of Less Favourable Treatment) Regulations 2002. Special conditions apply to apprenticeship contracts in terms of redundancy and dismissal. All contracts of employment must clearly state the length of the programme (and/or the qualification to be achieved), and unless an apprentice is in serious breach of contract, the programme cannot be terminated early (see Chapter 16 for more information about these regulations). This includes situations in which an employer tries to make an apprentice redundant owing to the economic downturn.

Summary

The structure, funding and working contracts and conditions of apprenticeships vary, depending on the type and level of apprenticeship. Young people who are taking part in Young Apprenticeships and Programme-Led Apprenticeships receive government funding to pay for their training, and may receive a personal training allowance, but are not paid a wage and are not subject to the usual working contractual conditions. Other apprentices are paid a wage by their employer and their work is subject to any relevant employment legislation. Government funding for training within these apprenticeship programmes depends on the type of apprenticeship, the age of the apprentice and the sector. Apprenticeship programmes vary in length depending on the type and the capabilities of the apprentice.

This section of the book has discussed the background to apprenticeships and provided practical information about the levels that are available and how they work. The next section will go on to provide information for students and adult learners, so that they can make a decision about whether an apprenticeship is right for them.

Further information

http://nationalemployerservice.org.uk

This is the website of the National Employer Service (NES), which 'provides impartial, specialist advice on apprenticeships exclusively to national, multi-site employers with more than 5,000 employees, supported by a direct funding contract'. NES employers currently deliver 20 per cent of all England's apprenticeships. If you are a large employer, visit this site for more information about how the service can help you.

Part Two
Information for students and adult learners

Chapter Four
Is an apprenticeship right for you?

The first section of this book provided background information about the modern-day apprenticeship scheme. This section of the book goes on to provide information for students (including school and college leavers) and adult learners.

Now that you understand more about apprenticeships, you need to start to think about whether undertaking an apprenticeship programme is suitable for you, personally. To do this effectively you need to seek appropriate advice and guidance, undertake a self-evaluation, balance your needs and wants, consider the practicalities and assess the positive and negative points about taking part in such a programme. These issues are discussed in this chapter.

Seeking advice and guidance

The case studies presented in Appendix 3 illustrate the importance of seeking advice and guidance about jobs and careers. This type of advice can be offered both on an informal basis and on a professional basis; often it is useful to obtain both types so that you can receive balanced and unbiased guidance.

Informal advice

Informal advice tends to be offered by friends and family, as we can see in Laura's case study (see Appendix 3). This advice may be useful because these people know you well and can offer advice about what they think would be best for you. However, informal advice can be influenced by personal opinions and biases: consider, for example, pushy parents who may think that you should be working towards a difficult qualification that stretches you too far and causes stress and unhappiness. Or perhaps an older sibling suggests that you follow their career route because it is something that they have enjoyed, even though you would not enjoy this type of career.

While it can be useful to listen to and take note of informal advice from friends and family, it is important to balance this type of advice with that offered by an experienced professional. This is because a professional adviser will be able to look at the wider picture and not be influenced by personal biases.

Professional advice

In general there are two types of professional advice. The first is 'tied' advice, which is offered by someone working for a particular organization. For example, you might decide to visit your local FE college or training provider to find out what apprenticeship programmes they run. The adviser will be able to offer you advice about all their programmes, but might not give advice about programmes that are offered elsewhere, even if these may be more suited to your needs. If you have decided that you only wish to study at this one college or training provider, perhaps for practical travel reasons, then this type of advice will be useful.

However, if you wish to weigh up all the possible options it is preferable to seek guidance from a professional who is able to offer advice about all the options that are available. For young people this type of service is offered by school careers advisers and careers services (details below). If you are an adult you can obtain professional advice from your local careers service (see Next Step details, below) or from your local Job Centre Plus, if you are currently out of work (see Chapter 13).

Michael illustrates in Appendix 3 that the standard of careers advice can vary considerably, so if you are not happy with the advice that you have received, or you feel that you have not been able to move forward with your decisions, you should try an alternative source. General careers advice can be obtained from the websites and telephone numbers listed below, by arranging an appointment with an adviser at your local careers centre, or through schools and youth clubs. Advice and guidance specifically about apprenticeships can be obtained from the NAS (**www.apprenticeships.org.uk**) and from other organizations listed in Chapter 6.

CASE STUDY

Careers advice was negligible to non-existent. From the village primary school, we were regarded as nothing better than prospective farm hands, tractor mechanics or gardeners. I was a bit of a surprise to some of the secondary teachers as I had an interest in science, geography and art! The geography teacher was the one who tried to guide me towards the army as he was my cadet officer.

SOURCE Ian Brooke, Weymouth, apprentice 1958–63, via e-mail

Undertaking a self-evaluation

If you are unsure about whether an apprenticeship is an appropriate pro-gramme to undertake, you may find it useful to carry out a self-evaluation. This involves thinking about your current skills, knowledge and experience, weighing up your likes and dislikes, thinking about what you like to do and what you would like to be doing in the future. The following questions will help you to undertake a self-evaluation:

- What skills do you have? Don't just think of obvious skills that may have developed from school, such as reading skills, but think about other skills that could have developed from a variety of situations. For example, you might have a wide circle of loyal friends – why is this? It is probably because you have good listening skills, good social skills and are able to get on well with a group of people. This illustrates that you may have good group-work skills or good teamwork skills, which are both valuable to employers.

- What hobbies and interests do you have? Is it possible to embark on a career that enables you to make use of these hobbies and interests? Are apprenticeships available that would help you to do this?

- What work experience do you have? Have you completed any part-time, voluntary, vacation or full-time employment in the past? Did you like the work? If yes, why did you enjoy it? If not, why didn't you enjoy it? This will help you to think more about the type of work that you would enjoy.

- What learning/training experience do you have? This can include all learning that has taken place in a formal setting, such as school and college, but also learning that has taken place in an informal setting, such as sports or hobbies. Think about when your learning has been successful and when it has been unsuccessful and work out why this was the case. For example, successful learning tends to take place when you are interested in the course, when you understand its relevance to your life, when you get on with the tutor/teacher and others in the class and when you feel comfortable in the learning environment. On the other hand, unsuccessful learning can occur when you are unhappy in the learning environment, when you are not interested in what you are learning and when you cannot understand the relevance of what you are learning.

- What jobs do you think you would like? When answering this question, think about specific aspects of the job, such as working hours, salary, working conditions, place of work and the tasks that you will be expected to undertake. Are apprenticeships available within the sector that interests you?

- What jobs do you think you would dislike? Again, think about specific aspects of the job. An honest appraisal will help you to filter out jobs/apprenticeships that would not suit you, personally.

- Do you have any ambitions or goals that you would like to attain in the future? What do you have to do to attain these goals? For example, you might want to obtain a Level 2 qualification in something that interests you. How can you achieve this? Can you do it through the apprenticeship route or would you be better getting a full-time job or studying full-time at college (see Chapter 5 for more information about assessing the alternatives to an apprenticeship programme)?

Balancing your needs and wants

When you undertake a self-evaluation you need to balance your needs and wants. At the very basic level, 'needs' include all those things that you require to live: food, drink, shelter and warmth (including clothing). When you think about whether an apprenticeship is a suitable route for you it is important to make sure that you will be able to meet all your basic needs.

As we saw in Chapter 1, there was a time when apprentices were provided with clothing, food and accommodation. Although some apprenticeships (such as those in the leisure industry) do still provide a uniform and accommodation, in most cases these are things that you will have to pay for from your salary. Perhaps your highest expense, when you begin an apprenticeship, will be accommodation so you need to make sure that you will have enough to pay for this on the wage that you are offered. Or, as the case studies in Appendix 3 illustrate, you need supportive parents who can provide cheap or free accommodation until you are able to pay your own way.

You may find that some of the more popular apprenticeships are not as well paid as others, and this is where you will need to balance your needs and wants. Although you may want to undertake a particular apprenticeship programme, you will need to make sure that you have enough money on which to live. When making these decisions you should note that many apprentices are offered a smaller starting salary, but that wages increase as you progress through the programme (see Chapter 3).

CASE STUDY

No, I have no problems, I mean I have to pay for my car insurance which is quite a lot and then I have the maintenance on my car, the petrol, the tax, MOTs and everything like that. And my parents are really supportive, I live at home, they don't expect me to pay rent so that's another big factor. So I'm trying to save money, I can save money, so it's no problem to me.

SOURCE Laura, business and administration apprentice, Weymouth

Considering the practicalities

When working out whether an apprenticeship programme is the right route for you to take, you also have to consider practical issues. Perhaps the most important of these is the availability of suitable apprenticeships in your area. As we can see from Michael's case study in Appendix 3, there are locations within the UK that have very few apprenticeships on offer (these tend to be rural locations). If none are offered in your locality, are you prepared to travel further afield? Can you afford to do so? Or are you happy to move to a new location if a suitable apprenticeship is not available in your area? If you are an adult with a family, is it possible and practical to move? Will you receive a high enough salary to make this move financially viable?

CASE STUDY

We've had a couple drop out of college because they can't afford to pay the transport, so that's a big problem. They end up coming back here for support. So yes, transport is the main issue and job-wise as well, again, getting them to jobs, but that's what we're here for really, to try and find another route for them so that they don't just drop out again completely.

SOURCE Petra, trainer and adviser, The Rendezvous, Sherborne

Another practical issue to consider is that of age. As we have seen in Chapter 3, age discrimination rules do not apply to government funding for training. Therefore, full funding is only offered to apprentices aged 16–18. If you are an adult there may be no funding available for your training and you may be required to meet all costs yourself. Can you afford to do so? Will this financial outlay be worth it in the long run? Will you be able to make up for financial loss through receiving higher wages in the future? More information about age and funding for apprenticeships is provided in Chapter 13 and more information about salaries for apprentices is provided in Chapter 3.

Assessing the positive and negative points

During my research, apprentices were asked to list the good and bad points about undertaking an apprenticeship programme. The following lists are presented as a guide. However, you should note that all lists such as these are highly subjective. Indeed, one person's bad point could be another person's good point and vice versa.

Good points:

- You earn a wage from day one.
- You get training that is relevant to the job.
- You don't have to pay for your own training (although some adults might have to: see above).
- You get a qualification *and* work experience.
- You get someone to look after you and make sure that you are happy and doing well.

- You get to meet other apprentices when you go to the training centre and you can have a good time.
- You might be offered a permanent job at the end.

Bad points:

- You don't get paid much.
- If you are an adult you might have to pay for your own training or even work unpaid (see Appendix 3).
- You have to do your training whether you like it or not.
- You have to get up early to get to work.
- You have to do a lot of work to pass your assessments (this can vary: see Chapter 6).
- You've got to pay tax and National Insurance.
- You might not get paid travel expenses and travel can be expensive.
- There can be problems with the funding, which can cause stress.
- You aren't guaranteed a job at the end.

Positive and negative experiences on apprenticeship programmes depend on a number of factors, including the personalities and motivation levels of the apprentices; the support, help and guidance offered by employers, work colleagues and tutors/trainers; the working and training environments; the salary level, perks and benefits offered. These are all important issues to consider when you are thinking about joining an apprenticeship programme.

Problems can be minimized if you are able to meet your prospective employer, visit the work premises, meet your tutor/trainer and visit the training premises. This may not always be possible but if you are able to do this you will be able to get more of a feel for whether the apprenticeship is right for you. More information about how to do this is provided in Chapters 6 and 7.

CASE STUDY

The Co-operative has set up the Co-operative Apprenticeship Academy, which is a new £9 million scheme that will benefit 2,000 young people. The Academy was launched first of all in the Farms section, with other businesses expected to follow suit in 2011.

The Co-operative Farms' new agricultural apprenticeship scheme is based across six of their farms. Placements are available on fruit farms in Hereford and vegetable farms at

Wisbech. There are also placements available in Cirencester, Daventry and Coldstream. Students will get the chance to complete an agricultural NVQ up to Level 3, with support from Reaseheath College in Cheshire (the training provider for the scheme). For more information about this scheme, visit **www.co-operative.coop/farms/careers/apprenticeship**. For more information about Reaseheath College, visit **www.reaseheath.ac.uk**.

Summary

The best way to find out whether an apprenticeship programme is right for you is to seek expert advice from a professional. These people will be able to talk to you about all the available options and help to steer you in the right direction. You may also find it useful to listen to informal advice from friends and family. In addition to this advice you should undertake a self-evaluation that helps you to think about your existing skills and experience, and helps you to work out how you would like your career to develop in the future. When doing this you need to think about practical issues, such as how you intend to meet your basic needs and the availability of apprenticeships in the locality. It is also important to think about the possible positive and negative aspects of taking part in an apprenticeship programme.

Once you have thought about these issues you can begin to think more about your options. Although you may be interested in becoming an apprentice, it is important to have an awareness of the alternatives that are available, as these will help you to choose the most appropriate route. These issues are discussed in the following chapter.

Further information

www.direct.gov.uk/en/YoungPeople
This section of the government information website provides information and advice for people aged 13–19. You can contact a careers adviser through this website by phone, e-mail or text and can use the chat room and message board to obtain more information and advice about apprenticeships, courses and careers.

www.careers-scotland.org.uk

This is the website of Careers Scotland. More information about Modern Apprenticeships in Scotland can be obtained from this site, along with information about researching a career and applying for jobs. Alternatively, you can obtain more information and advice by telephoning 0845 8 502 502.

www.careerswales.com

This is the website of Careers Wales. More information about apprenticeships in Wales can be obtained from the 16–19 section of this site, and there is a useful 'Apprenticeship Matching Service' available for those who wish to find an apprenticeship in Wales. Alternatively, you can telephone 0800 100 900 or e-mail the service for advice and guidance.

www.careersserviceni.com

This is the website of Careers Service Northern Ireland. Visit this site for information about apprenticeships in Northern Ireland and for general careers advice. There is a useful section for parents on this site.

https://nextstep.direct.gov.uk

This is the website of Next Step, which provides careers advice for adults in England. The website contains information about planning a career, undertaking an apprenticeship and funding further study. You can e-mail an adviser or telephone 0800 100 900 for specific advice and guidance or to arrange a face-to-face meeting.

Chapter Five
Assessing the alternatives

As we have seen, apprenticeships offer the opportunity to obtain full-time employment and work towards recognized qualifications within your chosen occupation. However, there are other education and career routes that you can take, such as enrolling at an FE college, applying to university, studying for vocational qualifications, taking part in work-based learning schemes or obtaining a full-time job that is not part of an apprenticeship scheme. When deciding whether an apprenticeship is the most appropriate programme for you, it is important to consider these alternative routes, which are discussed in this chapter.

Enrolling on an FE course

'Further education' is a term that refers to education that is undertaken after the compulsory school leaving age (currently 16 in all parts of the UK, although there are plans to increase this to 18 by 2015). Qualifications at this level include A levels, BTECS and NVQs up to Level 3 (see below). There are various types of organization offering courses at FE level:

- FE colleges, tertiary colleges and community colleges. These colleges offer a wide range of courses to students of all ages. Courses can be during the day, during the evening, full-time, part-time, day release or block release. Qualifications can be academic or vocational. You can obtain details of your local FE college by visiting the Association of Colleges website (details below).

- Sixth form colleges. These colleges are designed for 16–18-year-olds and tend to be attached to schools. Courses tend to run during normal school hours and qualifications can be academic or vocational. You can find your local sixth form college by using the directory available at **http://schoolsfinder.direct.gov.uk**.

- Specialist colleges. These colleges specialize in offering further education in specific subject areas such as art and design, agriculture, music or childcare. Courses can be full-time or part-time and some courses are residential with a bursary included. More information about these colleges and bursaries can be obtained from **http://moneytolearn.direct.gov.uk/residentialbursary**.

- Adult residential colleges. These colleges specialize in offering both short- and long-term courses for adults in a supportive, residential environment. Most colleges define adults as over the age of 21 and some will not offer places on their long courses to anyone who has already achieved qualifications at HE level. More information about these colleges can be obtained from **www.arca.uk.net**.

- Adult education service. Many local authorities run their own adult education service. These provide courses aimed specifically at adults. Some may lead to vocational qualifications, others to academic qualifications, or many courses are offered for interest, without leading to a specific qualification. Contact your local authority direct for information about their adult education services.

- Distance learning, correspondence learning and online courses. These courses provide the opportunity to learn in your home at a pace that suits you. There are many learning providers that offer distance learning courses, but you should check that they are accredited before enrolling by visiting the Open and Distance Learning Quality Council website (**www.odlqc.org.uk**). This site contains useful advice about choosing a course, knowing about costs and knowing what to do if things go wrong. It also lists, and provides contact details of, all accredited distance learning providers.

FE subject areas

There are a wide variety of courses available at FE level. These include:

- trades (eg plumbing, electrical, construction, hairdressing);
- crafts/hobbies (eg cookery, painting, decorating);

- health/fitness (eg yoga, martial arts, meditation);
- humanities (eg history, literature, geography, religion, philosophy);
- social sciences (eg sociology, psychology, economics);
- natural sciences (eg chemistry, physics, earth sciences);
- formal sciences (eg computing, maths, statistics);
- applied sciences (eg engineering, surveying, environmental studies);
- professions (eg health, social care, childcare).

You can find a suitable FE course by using the search facility available at **www.hotcourses.com**. Alternatively, you can find a local college prospectus by entering your postcode in the search box available at **http://yp.direct.gov.uk/ 14-19prospectus**.

Enrolling on an HE course

'Higher education' refers to education carried out at a level higher than A levels or Level 3. It tends to be delivered in universities or colleges of higher education, although some FE colleges and adult residential colleges may offer some HE courses such as the first year of a degree course or foundation degrees.

HE institutions provide the opportunity to study for a number of different qualifications. Generally, you can study for foundation degrees, undergraduate degrees, diplomas or postgraduate qualifications (this refers to any qualifications higher than the level of degree, such as Master's degrees or doctorates). There are also a number of professional qualifications for which you can study, including law, social work, teaching and engineering qualifications, at both undergraduate and postgraduate level.

Applying to university

The Universities and Colleges Admissions Service (UCAS) is the organization through which students make their application to university (details below). On their website you can access details of colleges and universities throughout the UK. There are hundreds of subjects available at HE level. An alphabetical list of all available subjects can be found by using the course search facility available on the UCAS website (click on 'course search' and then on 'search by subject' to access the list of subjects).

If you are thinking about going to university, you should note that not all applicants are accepted and you will have to obtain high entry grades to improve your chances. For example, in Scotland in 2010 Glasgow University announced its decision to raise entry requirements to four A grades at Higher in one sitting. This move disappointed a number of head teachers in Scotland because it was felt that it would disadvantage students from poorer backgrounds. However, a Glasgow University spokesperson said that the move was necessary because of increased demand (owing to fewer jobs available because of the economic downturn) and a cut in places and expected budget cuts. The university tends to have around 3,500 undergraduate places available each year, but has over 30,000 applicants for these places, at present.

In England, 688,310 people applied to start degree courses in October 2010 but only 479,057 were accepted, according to UCAS. This means that over 200,000 people who applied to university in 2010 were unsuccessful in their application. Therefore, if you are thinking of entering university you must try to improve your chances by obtaining high grades and making a successful application (see Further reading, below). Also, you need to be aware of the costs involved for university study and more information about this is provided in Chapter 9.

Taking vocational qualifications

The term 'vocational', when relating to qualifications, refers to those that are directly related to a person's present or future occupation. There are a variety of vocational qualifications available in the UK. These are described below.

OCR Nationals

OCR Nationals offer an exam-free alternative to GCSEs and are available at Levels 1 to 3. They are usually studied at school or college on either a full-time or part-time basis. These qualifications are mainly taken by learners over the age of 16, although some schools offer OCR Nationals at Levels 1 and 2 to 14- to 16-year-olds, normally in combination with other qualifications such as GCSEs or Key Skills.

All OCR Nationals help students develop their personal skills in areas relevant to the workplace, such as team working, communication and problem solving. The courses have been designed to accredit your achievements and ability to carry out tasks in a way that is relevant to the workplace. For more information about OCR Nationals, visit the OCR website (details below).

National Vocational Qualifications

NVQs are work-based qualifications in England, Wales and Northern Ireland that are achieved through assessment and training. In Scotland they are called Scottish Vocational Qualifications. If you are in paid or voluntary employment (full- or part-time), or you are at school or college with the opportunity for work placement, and you wish to improve your skills within your job, these qualifications may be of interest to you. As we have seen previously, NVQs can also be taken as part of an apprenticeship.

NVQs are based on a set of National Occupational Standards that describe the competencies or abilities expected in specific jobs. These reflect the skills and knowledge needed to do a job effectively, and show that you are competent in the area of work that the NVQ represents. They are offered at five levels, depending on the skills required for a particular job:

- NVQ Level 1: you will need to show that you are able to apply your skills and knowledge in a range of activities related to your job, most of which may be routine or predictable.

- NVQ Level 2: you will need to show that you are able to apply your skills and knowledge in a range of activities related to your job. Some of the activities will be complex or non-routine, and you may need to demonstrate that you can work on your own initiative and work well in a team or group.

- NVQ Level 3: you will need to show that you are able to apply your skills and knowledge in a broad range of activities related to your job. Most of these tasks are complex and non-routine. There is considerable responsibility and autonomy, and control or guidance of others is often required.

- NVQ Level 4: you will need to show that you can apply your knowledge and skills in a broad range of complex, technical or professional work activities performed in a wide variety of contexts and with a substantial degree of personal responsibility and autonomy. You may be responsible for the work of others and the allocation of resources.

- NVQ Level 5: you will need to demonstrate your knowledge and skills in a wide and often unpredictable variety of situations. You will have a great deal of personal autonomy and often significant responsibility for the work of others and for the allocation of substantial resources. You will have to demonstrate the ability to be able to analyse, diagnose, design, plan, execute and evaluate within your working role.

There are over 1,300 different NVQs to choose from and they are available in the vast majority of business sectors, ranging from business and management to manufacturing, production and engineering. NVQs have been designed so that they can be taken at a pace that suits you. This means that there is no set time-scale for their completion, although NVQs at Levels 1 and 2 tend to take around one year to complete, whereas NVQs at Level 3 may take around two years to complete. More information about NVQs can be obtained from the 'students and parents' section of the Office of Qualifications and Examinations Regulation (Ofqual) website: **www.ofqual.gov.uk**.

City & Guilds qualifications

The City & Guilds Group is a registered charity that was established in 1878 to encourage education and training in, and for, the workplace. It is the leading vocational awarding body in the UK, offering a wide variety of qualifications through approved centres worldwide. Qualifications can be gained in many sectors ranging from office-based and management qualifications to vehicle maintenance and hairdressing. More information about City & Guilds qualifications can be obtained from their website (details below).

BTEC qualifications

BTEC qualifications are work-related qualifications, available in a wide range of subjects. They are usually studied at college on either a full-time or part-time basis by people over the age of 16. If you are interested in gaining qualifications while learning more about a particular sector or industry, these qualifications may be of interest to you. BTECs can be taken as part of an apprenticeship programme.

BTECs are designed as specialist qualifications for students who have a clear view of their future career, or are wishing to progress to higher education, and/or are hoping to improve their professional qualifications. They are available at the following levels on the National Qualifications Framework (NQF):

- NQF Level 1: BTEC Introductory Diplomas and Certificates (equivalent to GCSEs grades D – G);

- NQF Level 2: BTEC First Diplomas and Certificates (equivalent to GCSEs grades A* – C);

- NQF Level 3: BTEC Diplomas, Certificates and Awards (equivalent to A levels and are recognized by universities and FE colleges for entry purposes);
- NQF Level 4: BTEC Professional Diplomas, Certificates and Awards (equivalent to HNCs and HNDs);
- NQF Levels 5 and 6: BTEC Advanced Professional Diplomas, Certificates and Awards (equivalent to various professional qualifications).

More information about BTECs can be obtained from the Edexcel website (details below). You can use the BTEC National Centre Finder on this website to locate schools and colleges offering BTEC Nationals. More information about the NQF can be obtained from **www.ofqual.gov.uk**.

Foundation degrees

Foundation degrees were set up in 2001–02 and were designed as a new two-year HE qualification that could be completed quicker than a conventional degree, especially for people who were reluctant, or unable, to take too much time from work for their studies.

Foundation degrees are offered by universities in partnership with HE colleges and FE colleges and have been designed to give people the technical and professional skills that are needed by employers. They combine academic study with workplace learning and take two years to complete on a full-time basis or three to four years on a part-time basis. There are hundreds of courses available, covering a diverse range of subject areas, and study methods are flexible to enable people in work to fit their studies around their work commitments. There are no set entry requirements for these degrees: staff at the college/university that you choose will decide whether you are eligible and will take into account your previous work experience. There is a database available to help you to find a foundation degree suitable for your needs (details below).

Foundation degrees may be of interest to you if you wish to continue in part-time or full-time employment while you are studying. They can be related directly to your work or they could be in a different subject that may help you to change careers at a later date. They can also be of interest to people who are seeking work, as they provide the opportunity to study on a vocational course that will enhance your chances of finding work, or enable you to transfer to a full degree course if you enjoy, and succeed in, your studies. Some companies enable you to undertake a foundation degree as part of an apprenticeship programme.

Learning and earning opportunities

If you are interested in work-based learning, but wish to consider alternatives to the apprenticeship scheme or the vocational qualifications outlined above, there are a number of schemes available. These depend on your age, employment status and the type of education and training that appeals to you.

Time off for study and training

This scheme is aimed at young people aged 16–17 who are in paid employment and who wish to improve their skills. It is available in all parts of the UK and has been designed to help improve the skills and qualifications of young people who have entered jobs that offer little education and training.

The amount of time that you can have off work depends on the course requirements and the needs of your employer and their business. You will need to discuss this with your employer and reach an agreement with which you are both happy. Your employer must give you 'reasonable' time off work, and, although there are no set limits as to what constitutes 'reasonable', it is taken to mean around one day a week, depending on your course and your needs. More information about this scheme can be obtained from **www.direct.gov.uk/en/EducationAndLearning**.

Skillseekers (Scotland)

This programme is available to young people aged 16–19 living in Scotland who wish to develop their skills and improve their qualifications. It is open to young people who are no longer in full-time education at school or college and is available both for people who are already in work and those who are seeking work. Skillseekers vocational training helps to provide you with improved practical skills by supporting you as you work towards an SVQ or NVQ Level 2 or 3 when a Modern Apprenticeship is not available. More information about this scheme can be obtained from **www.skillsdevelopmentscotland.co.uk**.

Trade union funding

If you are in paid employment and you are a member of a trade union or a union representative or officer, you may be able to receive subsidized or free education and training while you are earning a wage. All representatives or union officers have the legal right to reasonable paid time off during working hours for trade union duties, which includes training (if your employer recognizes the union for collective bargaining). If you are an ordinary member of a union you should be entitled to some paid time off work if you do not have any qualifications above Level 2. Also, some employers will enable you to take paid time off for qualifications above this level, especially if the qualification is work related. Contact your union representative for more information.

The Learning Through Work Scheme

This scheme is available for people who are interested in obtaining a university-level qualification. It enables you to study without leaving your job and is of benefit to the organization for which you work and helps you to progress in your personal career. Learning takes place using projects you complete as part of your current working role and tutor support is provided interactively online and face-to-face. This means that all your learning takes place in the workplace and that you do not need to attend a university or college to learn. Visit **www.learningthroughwork.org** for more information about this scheme.

Obtaining full-time employment

Another option that is available to you is to obtain a full-time job that is not part of an apprenticeship programme. If you do this you will receive a salary that is at least the National Minimum Wage and you could also receive other benefits and perks, such as the opportunity to join a pension scheme. If you do decide to obtain full-time employment it is still possible to continue your training and obtain qualifications if you wish (see some of the work-based learning schemes, described above). If you are interested in obtaining full-time employment, visit the jobseekers' database, which can be found at **http://jobseekers.direct.gov.uk**.

Summary

When assessing whether an apprenticeship programme is the right choice for you, it is important to consider the alternatives. There are various work-based schemes available, other than apprenticeships. Also, there are full-time and part-time education opportunities available at both FE and HE level. This chapter has provided information about all these schemes to help you to make an informed choice.

If, after having read this chapter, you wish to continue down the apprenticeship route, you need to think more about which apprenticeship is right for you. These issues are discussed in the following chapter.

Further information

www.ucas.com

UCAS is the organization responsible for managing applications to HE courses in the UK. On this website you can find all the information you need about applying for higher education. There is a useful student budget calculator available that will help you to work out the costs involved in university study.

http://fd.ucas.com

More information about foundation degrees can be obtained from this site. There is a useful course search facility to help you to find a foundation degree course that is suitable for your needs. You can search by subject group, study mode, institution and/or region.

www.cityandguilds.com

This is the City & Guilds website. Here you can find more information about City & Guilds qualifications, use the qualifications finder to find qualifications suitable for your needs and find out about regional Apprenticeship Summits. These offer the opportunity for businesses, politicians and education leaders to get together to discuss apprenticeships and their importance to the UK's economy.

www.edexcel.com

This is the website of Edexcel, the awarding body of BTEC qualifications. On this site there is a section for students, which includes information about the qualifications that you can work towards. The site also provides useful information on study options in the UK and overseas, along with tips on taking and passing examinations. You can use the BTEC National Centre Finder to locate schools and colleges offering BTEC Nationals in your area.

www.ocrnationals.com

This is the website of the awarding body for OCR Nationals. On this site you can find more information about the different levels of qualifications and view case studies about OCR Nationals. You can also access their 'career path finder' which enables you to match careers with your OCR qualifications.

www.sqa.org.uk

This is the website of the Scottish Qualifications Authority, the national body in Scotland responsible for the development, accreditation, assessment and certification of qualifications other than degrees. Here you can find further information about SVQs, Modern Apprenticeships and other types of education and training in Scotland.

www.aoc.co.uk

This is the website of the Association of Colleges. On this site you can access contact details of all FE colleges in the UK.

www.scotlandscolleges.ac.uk

Scotland's Colleges has been established to support, represent and promote the Scottish College sector. You can find out more information about further education in Scotland by visiting this site.

www.anic.ac.uk

This is the website of the Association of Northern Ireland Colleges. You can find out more about further education in Northern Ireland and link to all the colleges from this site.

www.jobcentreplus.gov.uk

Jobcentre Plus is a government agency that is part of the Department for Work and Pensions (DWP). Its role is to support people of working age from welfare into work and to help to fill vacancies advertised by employers. You can use the postcode search facility on the website to find contact details of your nearest Jobcentre Plus office.

http://jobseekers.direct.gov.uk

You can search for jobs, training, careers, childcare and voluntary work using the search facility on this site. You can search by job type and geographical location. Each entry contains a description of the job, wages, working hours, date posted, pension details, application procedures and employer contact details.

www.jobcentreonline.com

If you live in Northern Ireland you can use this search facility to find job vacancies in your area.

Further reading

Stannard, I (2010) *How to Write a Winning UCAS Personal Statement*, 2nd edn, Trotman Publishing, Richmond

Chapter Six
Choosing the right apprenticeship scheme

O nce you have assessed the alternatives and decided that an apprenticeship is the right route to take, you need to find out what is available and work out which programme would be the most suitable. To do this effectively you need to know where to find information about the different types of apprenticeship and register to receive information quickly so that you can get ahead of your competitors. You also need to find out about potential employers and know how to make the most effective choices. These issues are discussed in this chapter. (For a list of all the different types of apprenticeship that are available, and the job roles within each of these programmes, see Appendix 1.)

Finding out what is available

There are various sources of information that you can use to find a suitable apprenticeship programme. These are discussed below.

Online information

Online directories, databases and search facilities are available to help you to find out about apprenticeship vacancies. The most useful sites are:

https://apprenticeshipvacancymatchingservice.lsc.gov.uk

This apprenticeship vacancy service is available for anyone who is looking for an apprenticeship in England (there are links available on the home page to other parts of the UK). You can search the database by occupation type/job role, keyword, learning provider, vacancy reference number, postcode and location. It is also possible to search by the date that vacancies were posted and the amount of weekly wage offered. You will need to register to view the results of your search. If you are already in employment, or wish to undertake a college-based apprenticeship, you can use this search facility to find a local organization/college that provides apprenticeship training.

www.mappit.org.uk

This service is available for anyone looking for a Modern Apprenticeship in Scotland. On the home page you can specify the type of sector that you would like to work in, the area of specialism within that sector and the location in which you would like to work. It is also possible to view an alphabetical listing of all apprenticeships. You can apply for apprenticeship vacancies using this service.

www.careerswales.com/16to19

Visit this section of the Careers Wales website to access the Apprenticeship Matching Service. At time of writing this is a new service that offers information about vacancies only in certain parts of Wales. However, it is hoped that the service will be available in all parts of Wales once the system has been tested. If you want to apply for a vacancy using this service you need to upload your 'Apprenticeship Profile', which is similar to a CV (curriculum vitae) and provides information to prospective employers. You need to register your details to use this system.

www.careersserviceni.com

If you are looking for an apprenticeship in Northern Ireland there is not an apprenticeship matching service available. However, you can visit the Careers Service Northern Ireland website for information about apprenticeship vacancies. You can also visit your local Jobs and Benefits Office/Job Centre for information about vacancies or visit **www.jobcentreonline.com** which may, from time to time, carry apprenticeship vacancies.

www.opendoorsmedia.co.uk

This site is available for people living in England. Click on the area in which you live to access your Regional Training Prospectus. Here you can find out about the wide variety of training opportunities that are available, including information about apprenticeships. You can also sign up to receive the Open Doors newsletter, which contains information about job opportunities and regional learning and training opportunities.

www.apprentices.co.uk

If you are interested in an engineering apprenticeship, visit this site to find out about vacancies in your area. You can register your details and apply for vacancies online.

www.notgoingtouni.co.uk

This site provides details of the various options that are available for people who don't want to go to university. It includes information about Apprentice-ships, Advanced Apprenticeships, gap years and various types of learning opportunity. You can search the database by type of job/training and by keyword.

National Apprenticeship Week

In 2011 National Apprenticeship Week began on 7 February. During this week there were apprenticeship fairs held all over the UK, local and national media covered a wide variety of stories and webcasts were available from the NAS website (**www.apprenticeships.org.uk**). Find out when the next National Apprenticeship Week is to be held and make sure that you keep abreast of what is available on both a local and national level. Dates will be announced on the NAS website.

Apprenticeship fairs and open days

As we have seen above, there are a variety of apprenticeship fairs that are staged during National Apprenticeship Week. However, there are fairs and open days available throughout the year. Times and dates vary, so contact your local college or training provider for more information about what is available in your area. You can also contact your local ATA or GTA for more information (see Chapter 1 for contact details).

Job Centres and careers services

As we saw in Chapter 4, face-to-face careers advice and guidance is available from trained professionals. Often this is a good way to get advice tailored to your needs. These people can also offer advice about specific apprenticeship vacancies in the area in which you live. Consult the list provided in Appendix 1 of this book and discuss programmes that are of interest to you with your careers adviser to find out whether vacancies are available. See Chapter 4 for information about contacting your local careers advisory service.

Trade, craft and professional associations

Many trades, crafts and professions have an association that acts as an umbrella group within the sector, providing a variety of services that can include advertising, training, political lobbying and publishing. Some of these associations advertise jobs for employers within their sector, so you can contact the association direct or visit their website to find out whether they are advertising any apprenticeship vacancies.

Journals and trade magazines

If you are interested in a particular trade or profession, find out whether there are any journals or magazines that are related specifically to your chosen sector. Often these publications contain advertisements for jobs and apprenticeships, along with useful articles about careers within these sectors. Again, many will have an online presence so check whether this is the case to avoid costs associated with buying publications.

Sector Skills Councils

As we saw in Chapter 1, SSCs are state-sponsored, employer-led organizations that cover specific economic sectors in the UK and devise the frameworks for apprenticeships within their sector. If you are interested in a specific sector visit the relevant SSC website (contact details for each SSC are provided in Appendix 5).

Some SSC websites contain information about apprenticeship vacancies, some link to organizations offering vacancies and some have set up additional websites that offer careers advice and information for people hunting for apprenticeships or jobs within their sector. Most also contain information about job and occupation roles within their sector, including case studies. For example, e-skills UK, the SSC for business and information technology, has set up two websites: **www.bigambition.co.uk**, which provides insider information about careers in technology, and **www.bringitonni.info**, which provides careers information for young people in Northern Ireland.

Local and national newspapers

Local and national newspapers often contain jobs listings that, on occasions, include information about apprenticeships. Find out on which days of the week relevant job supplements appear; for example, the *Guardian* has the following:

Monday – media;

Tuesday – education;

Wednesday – public sector;

Thursday – information technology.

Newspapers also have their own websites that contain job listings. You may find the following sites useful:

http://jobs.guardian.co.uk

www.tesjobs.co.uk

www.jobs.telegraph.co.uk

www.jobs.telegraph.co.uk

www.timesonline.co.uk

Your local newspaper may also have job listings available online, so check whether this is the case before buying a copy of the newspaper. Remember that most public libraries hold copies of newspapers so you don't have to buy a copy if you cannot afford to do so.

Getting ahead of competitors

To get ahead of competitors you need to know about vacancies as soon as they become available. Some of the services listed above enable you to register your details and receive free e-mail and/or text message alerts about new vacancies. If this service is available, register as soon as possible, providing specific information about the type of apprenticeship that interests you. Once you receive an e-mail or text message, act quickly so that you can keep one step ahead of competitors.

Other services enable you to register your details and they will carry out a matching service for you. Again, register with these organizations, providing as much information as possible, and make sure that you act quickly on any messages sent from prospective employers. Ensure that you have an up-to-date CV to hand and that you can provide employers with all information quickly and easily (see Chapter 7). You should also make sure that you have references available or that you have approached two people who can act as referees at short notice (see Chapter 7).

During my research for this book I spoke to an employer who said that if young people have applied for a position they should try to make sure that they answer the telephone when prospective employers contact them. Employers don't want to speak to parents and consider candidates to be 'more mature' if they answer the 'phone and speak direct to the employer.

Finally, if you do contact an employer or register your details, you may not hear anything back (some employers have too many applications and cannot respond to all, and others, unfortunately, don't see the importance of responding to enquiries; see case study, below). Therefore, the more applications and enquiries you make the better your chances of hearing back from an employer.

CASE STUDY

I Googled apprenticeships and it came up with the National Apprenticeship website so I signed on to that and I had a look at the vacancies in the area. I applied for a couple and didn't hear anything back, they were for basic admin assistants. But I didn't hear anything back from them, and then it got to December time and I was still at Debenhams and I hadn't heard back from any apprenticeships and I hadn't had any feedback so I was kind of panicking, so I had no guidance.

SOURCE Laura, Business and Administration Apprentice, Weymouth

Researching potential employers

If you think that you have found a suitable apprenticeship using any of the methods described above, you should try to find out more about the employer before you make an application. This is important because it will help you to make sure that they are reliable, trustworthy, a good person/organization to work for and that they will help you to complete your apprenticeship successfully. This includes providing a good mentor and making sure that you have the necessary time off and support for your training.

Researching online

A good place to start your research is to conduct an online search. This involves a careful viewing of the employer's website and a search for any other mention of the employer, such as in personal blogs, forums or chat rooms. When doing this you must make sure that you analyse the information carefully so that you can make judgements about the reliability of what you are reading (see below).

Face-to face meetings

Try to meet prospective employers, if possible. Although you will probably have to do this during a formal interview (see Chapter 7), you should also try to meet them on an informal basis. Find out whether it would be possible to visit the organization before your interview takes place so that you can meet the employer and other employees. Also, try to have a chat with other apprentices if there are any working for the organization. This will enable you to have a full discussion about all the aspects of working for the employer and give you a much better idea as to whether the apprenticeship is the right choice and would suit your needs.

Ensuring information is reliable

Use all avenues available to you to find out information about prospective employers, but make sure that you undertake a careful critique and analysis of the information that you find. This will help you to make judgements about the reliability of the information that is being presented. In general, information is presented in four ways: as statistics, facts, opinions and arguments.

- 'Statistics' is a numerical discipline that involves collecting, organizing, analysing, interpreting and presenting data. We also refer to the data that are presented as 'statistics'. The data are only as good as the methods used to create them and the skill of the statistician who collects the data. Figures can be misleading, incorrect (whether deliberate or by mistake) and open to misinterpretation. It is important to analyse all statistics about prospective employers carefully before taking them to be correct.

- 'Facts' are things that can be investigated and are found to be true. They tend to be exact and specific. However, not everything presented as a 'fact' is correct and true, so again, you need to check your sources and make sure that the information is valid and reliable before believing facts about prospective employers.

- 'Opinions' are personal beliefs or judgements that are not based on proof or certainty. People may have negative opinions about prospective employers that are based on personal grudges or bias, for example, or positive opinions could be posted by happy employees or biased family members. Therefore, you need to be aware of the reasons that people have for presenting their personal opinions before making your own judgements.

- 'Arguments' are reasons or explanations given to support or reject a point of view. It is up to you to work out whether an argument about a prospective employer (whether good or bad) has been backed up by adequate evidence. For example, a competitor may try to argue that their product is much better and that they treat their workers much more fairly, without presenting any evidence to back up this argument.

Making a decision

When you come to make your final decisions about what type of apprenticeship (and employer) is most suitable, you should consider the following points:

- Do you have the required aptitude, skills and talents to undertake the type of work that will be required (see Chapter 7)? Or do you have the ability to learn the appropriate skills and develop your talents as your apprenticeship progresses? For example, apprenticeships in the construction industry may require physical fitness, strength and manual dexterity, whereas office-based apprenticeships may require patience and good organization skills. If you are in doubt about this you should discuss the issues with a professional advice worker, your teachers/tutor and/or current employer (if relevant).

- Do you have enough personal interest in the work and in the training that will be required? Apprenticeships require hard work and dedication, and your motivation and enthusiasm will be easier to maintain if you have a strong personal interest in your work and training.

- Do you have any previous experience of the particular trade or profession? Or does a family member or friend have any personal experience in this area? You will be able to make a more informed choice if you have some personal experience on which to draw, or if you are able to have a full and frank discussion with someone who has experience of the type of work that you are considering.

- Are you absolutely sure that you understand what the apprenticeship entails? Some people make decisions based on incomplete knowledge or even a romantic notion of the role. You must make sure that you have all the facts: speak to employers, employees, family members, friends and trained advice workers. It may even be possible to undertake a short period of work placement before you commit to your apprenticeship. This will enable you to find out whether the work meets your expectations.

- Do you understand how much work, training and assessment is required? This is important as amounts can vary between apprenticeships, as the following quotation illustrates.

CASE STUDY

Well I've assessed people doing apprenticeships for years now. They are a bit hit and miss to be honest, depending on the workplace you go out to. For the young person, if they get a good placement, it's brilliant, you know. I think having internally verified some of the apprenticeships that are out there at the moment, particularly in hospitality and catering, they are so unwieldy. There is just far too much work involved for a young person. The number of units in their NVQ, they've then got to do their Key Skills, they've then got to do the Employer Rights and Responsibilities, they then have to do all their Technical Certificates on top of that. And it's huge, and then you look at something like, I don't know, customer care for example, which is probably a third of the size for the same-level qualification, so there's a lot of difference between which route you choose as to how much work you are going to have to do.

SOURCE Petra, trainer and adviser, The Rendezvous, Sherborne

Completing a choices checklist

The following checklist will help to ensure that you make the right choices when making decisions about a suitable apprenticeship. The more 'yes' answers you are able to give the better. If you answer 'no' to any questions, you may need to conduct some more research or have further discussions with a trained adviser to make sure that you choose the right apprenticeship.

	Yes	No
1 Have you sought advice from an experienced professional?	☐	☐
2 Have you found out all you can about the apprenticeship?	☐	☐
3 Have you found out all you can about the employer?	☐	☐
4 Have you met the employer?	☐	☐
5 Have you found out all you can about the training that will be required?	☐	☐
6 Have you met the trainer/assessor?	☐	☐
7 Have you visited the training premises?	☐	☐
8 Do you understand the assessment procedures for your training?	☐	☐
9 Will you be able to complete the required study?	☐	☐
10 Do you know what qualifications will be gained at the end of the programme?	☐	☐
11 Do you know what the job entails?	☐	☐
12 Do you understand what skills/talents will be required?	☐	☐
13 Do you have the necessary skills/talents or the ability to acquire them?	☐	☐
14 Do you have the necessary qualifications to make an application?	☐	☐
15 Do you know what salary will be paid?	☐	☐
16 Will the salary provide you with enough money to meet your basic needs?	☐	☐
17 Have you found out about any perks and benefits?	☐	☐
18 Do you understand what these perks and benefits entail?	☐	☐
19 Have you found out all you can about working conditions?	☐	☐

	Yes	No
20 Are you happy with the working conditions?	☐	☐
21 Have you had a chance to view your apprenticeship contract?	☐	☐
22 Do you understand the contract?	☐	☐
23 Are you happy to meet the terms of the contract?	☐	☐
24 Have you met any of the organization's employees/apprentices?	☐	☐
25 Do you think you will get on with the other employees/apprentices?	☐	☐
26 Do you know for how long you will be an apprentice?	☐	☐
27 Are you happy to spend this length of time on the programme?	☐	☐
28 Will this programme prepare you well for your future career?	☐	☐
29 Will you be given guidance about progression routes?	☐	☐

Summary

There are various sources of information about apprenticeship vacancies, such as online databases, job centres and careers services, trade associations and local and national media. Some of these services enable you to register your details and receive information about vacancies when they become available. It is important to register with relevant organizations so that you can receive information quickly and remain ahead of your competitors. When choosing an apprenticeship that is of interest you should try to find out more about the prospective employer before you make an application. It is also important to think about your existing experience, skills and talents when making a decision.

Once you have chosen an apprenticeship programme you can go on to make an application. Information about how to do this successfully is provided in the next chapter.

Chapter Seven
Applying for an apprenticeship

Once you have found an apprenticeship programme that is of interest, you need to go on to make an application. There are various methods of applying depending on the type of apprenticeship and the preferences of the employer. This includes applying online, filling in application forms and producing a CV. It is also possible to arrange to begin a programme with your current employer, without the need for a formal application. When applying you need to make the most of your previous experience and qualifications and know how to prepare for and attend interviews. These issues are discussed in this chapter.

Understanding the application process

The application process depends on a number of factors, including whether you are currently in employment or not, where you live in the UK, the type of apprenticeship and the application procedures adopted by prospective employers.

Applying online

As we saw in Chapter 6, some online services enable you to make your application online. This means that you have to complete only one application form that can then be sent to any employer that has an appropriate apprenticeship vacancy. Some of these online services will match your application automatically to appropriate employers, whereas others require you to search for, and send your details to, appropriate employers.

If you live in England you can apply through the National Apprenticeship Service (NAS) in the following way:

1 Go to **https://apprenticeshipvacancymatchingservice.lsc.gov.uk**.

2 Register your details.

3 Create a username and password.

4 Receive a confirmation e-mail and click on the link to activate your account.

5 Create your 'MyHome' page.

6 Search for an apprenticeship.

7 Browse your results.

8 Save your searches.

9 Find an apprenticeship.

10 Complete an application form.

11 Save your application form.

12 View the status of your application.

If you live in Scotland you can apply through Mappit in the following way:

1 Go to **www.mappit.org.uk**.

2 Use the search facility to find an apprenticeship scheme that interests you.

3 Make sure that they are recruiting.

4 Make sure that you have the necessary qualifications/experience.

5 Read application instructions.

6 If necessary, complete the brief online application form.

7 If necessary, attach your CV.

8 If necessary, apply direct to the employer, following the application guidelines.

If you live in Wales you can apply through Careers Wales in the following way:

1 Go to **www.careerswales.com/16to19**.

2 Click on the 'Apprenticeship Matching Service' link.

3 Register for the system.

4 Create a username and password.

5   Search for vacancies. (The system was set up in July 2010 and is running as a pilot scheme for a year, so there are only a few vacancies available at the present time. It is hoped that more will become available as time progresses.)

6   Complete an 'Apprenticeship Profile', which is like a CV. This is used if you wish to apply for vacancies. It will also be sent to employers who will be able to shortlist possible candidates and contact you if they wish to select you for interview.

As we saw in Chapter 6, at this time there is not a national database for all apprenticeships in Northern Ireland, so contact your local Jobs and Benefits Office/Job Centre or the Careers Service Northern Ireland website (**www.careersserviceni.com**) to find out about vacancies and application procedures in your area.

Applying to a new employer

As we saw in Chapter 6, some employers advertise in local or national newspapers and/or trade magazines. If this is the case you will need to apply for the apprenticeship in the way specified in the advertisement. This may involve completing an application form or sending your CV and covering letter (see below).

Applying to your current employer

If you already have a full-time or part-time job and wish to undertake an apprenticeship, it is possible to talk to your employer and convince them that this is a good route to take, both for you and for your employer. In this case you may not have to complete any additional application forms because you already are working for your employer. However, you may have to apply to a college/learning provider (see below).

Applying to a learning provider

If you are already in employment and your employer has agreed to support you through an apprenticeship programme, you will need to find a local learning provider that is able to arrange your training. Or, if you are not in work but are interested in an apprenticeship scheme that is based at college, you will need to find a local learning provider.

If you live in England, visit **https://apprenticeshipvacancymatchingservice. lsc.gov.uk** and use the learning provider search to find a suitable provider. You can search by occupation/job type and by location. Alternatively, you can enter the name of your local learning provider. Search results display the name of the learning provider, a link to their website and the sector success rate. If you live in other parts of the UK, visit the relevant careers websites listed in Chapter 4 for information about local learning providers. Although application procedures vary, in general, you will need to follow the procedure set out below.

1 Find a suitable programme using the methods described above.

2 Fill in an apprentice application form (usually available online or on paper).

3 Attend an initial assessment to determine your suitability for the course. At this stage you may be advised that a different training programme would better suit your needs.

4 If you are successful with the initial assessment you will be invited to an interview with a training and placement adviser (or with a training coordinator/assessor, depending on the procedures adopted by the learning provider) who will work with you to develop an action plan for training and employment.

5 After this interview you will be given provisional acceptance on an apprenticeship programme (providing a suitable employer can be found, if you are not already in employment).

Filling in an apprenticeship application form

When completing apprenticeship application forms (for employers or learning providers) you should take note of the following:

- Follow all application instructions carefully. If an employer asks only for an application form, don't send extra information, unless requested to do so.

- Research the employer/company and the apprenticeship, making sure that the information supplied on your application form is aimed specifically at that company and apprenticeship scheme (see Chapter 6).

- Make sure that all application forms are free from grammatical errors, spelling mistakes and typing mistakes. Ask someone to read through the information before you submit if you are in doubt.

- When completing online forms, check whether you have a save facility so that you can return to the form at a later date, saving and altering answers if needs be. If not, you might find it useful to practise answering questions before you complete the form. Make sure that you have all information easily to hand once you begin to fill in the form.

- If you have to fill in the form by hand, write neatly and clearly, using black ink. You might find it useful to photocopy the form and practise filling it in before you complete the original.

- If you are finding it difficult to answer some questions you could try viewing some sample questions and answers online, but make sure that you don't simply copy other answers (enter 'sample job application forms' into your search engine to be directed to relevant sites). Try to be truthful and honest as experienced employers can spot when candidates are exaggerating or lying. You may find it useful to seek advice from siblings, parents, teachers and careers advisers if you are struggling.

- Keep copies of all application forms so that you know what you have said if you are invited for interview.

Producing a CV

A CV is a short list of facts about you and your work history, skills and experience. It is sent to prospective employers so that they can assess your suitability for a vacancy and invite you for interview.

Today there are some very useful online tools that help you to produce a CV. Examples include the CV tools at **www.planitplus.net** and **https:// nextstep.direct.gov.uk**. Sample CVs can be found at **www.direct.gov.uk** (enter 'CV' into the search box to be directed to the right pages). You can use these online tools to build your own CV or to use a template to create your own.

CVs should contain the following information:

- your name;
- your address;

- your phone number;
- your e-mail address (if you have one);
- qualifications and training;
- your career history (including full-time, part-time and voluntary work);
- a personal profile (a short statement about yourself that can be adapted for each position that you apply for);
- personal achievements;
- interests, including sports and hobbies;
- additional information, such as career breaks, driving licence etc;
- names, addresses and telephone numbers of two references (make sure that these people are happy to be a referee before you include their information).

Make sure that all information is succinct and to the point. In general CVs should not be more than two pages long. Your CV should be neatly typed and printed on good quality paper. It should also be free from errors: ask someone to check it once you have produced a draft.

Writing a covering letter

When sending an application form or a CV it is good practice to include a covering letter. This is a short letter that should include the following:

- who you are;
- why you are applying for the apprenticeship;
- why you are interested in both the apprenticeship and the company;
- where you saw the apprenticeship advertised;
- why you think you are suitable for the apprenticeship.

The letter should be succinct (usually one page in length). It should not repeat what has been said in your CV or application form, but can expand on areas that are relevant to the apprenticeship that have not been covered elsewhere. Again, it should be neatly typed on good quality paper and free from mistakes. If possible, you should address the letter to a named person (this may involve contacting the company). Make sure that all your contact details are included in the letter.

Making the most of your previous experience

You have to sell yourself to prospective employers and you have to stand out from the crowd if you are to be offered a place on an apprenticeship programme. One of the ways that you can do this is to think carefully about your previous experience and make sure that you provide a succinct, relevant and interesting list for prospective employers.

Although you may be young and think that you don't have any previous experience, you can still include items on such a list. For example, if you are thinking about an apprenticeship in childcare you may not have experience of looking after other people's children, but you may have experience of looking after younger siblings. Think about practical tasks that you have undertaken, such as feeding, clothing and bathing them. Think about how you have helped them to learn, perhaps by teaching words or games. Have you helped them to understand when a situation may be dangerous, such as crossing roads and not eating things they find on the ground? All this is good, relevant experience that can be included in information supplied to a prospective childcare employer.

Remember that it is not just relevant work experience, but also relevant life experience. For example, perhaps you have encountered an emergency situation where you had to take control. This would imply that you can function well under extreme pressure and that you are organized and can keep a cool head. Or perhaps you have always enjoyed your own company and can keep yourself occupied and never get bored. This could suggest that you work well independently, using your own initiative and without the need for constant supervision.

Take time to think about all your previous experience because this is very important when filling in application forms. If you are struggling to come up with a suitable list, seek further help from siblings, parents, friends, teachers and/or professional advice workers.

Making the most of your qualifications

When thinking about your previous qualifications you need to list those you have obtained and show how they are useful to the apprenticeship for which you are applying. For example, if you have English qualifications you could demonstrate how this will help with your written work or your ability to communicate with others. Maths qualifications can help with any numerical tasks you may have to undertake during the apprenticeship.

If you do not have any previous qualifications you may need to think a little more laterally. For example, have you passed your driving test? This shows that you are able to follow procedures, understand rules and regulations and have good manual dexterity skills, in addition to that fact that you can drive, which might be a requirement of the apprenticeship. Or perhaps you have obtained some sports badges, trophies or team membership? This could illustrate that you are fit and healthy, are a good team (or individual) player, that you are dedicated and determined to succeed. All certificates, prizes and qualifications should be considered when you are thinking about what to include in your CV.

Preparing for interviews and assessments

If your application for an apprenticeship is successful, you will be invited to attend an interview and/or assessment. When preparing for this you should follow the procedure set out below:

1 Confirm that you are able to attend at the appointed time and date.

2 Find out all you can about the company and about the apprenticeship (see Chapter 6).

3 Read through a copy of your application form/CV to refresh your memory.

4 Think about all the questions that could be asked and practise answering each question (see further reading, below).

5 Think about awkward questions that could be asked and work through some possible answers.

6 Think about the ways in which your skills, knowledge and experience are suitable for the apprenticeship.

7 Think about questions that you would like to ask. An interview is not just about finding a suitable candidate – you need to make sure that the company and the apprenticeship programme are right for you. Think about what you need to know to find this out, but make sure that you ask questions in a sensible, polite manner. This could include asking questions about the training, your mentor and working conditions.

8   Practise the interview with a sibling, parent or friend. Play close attention to body language, eye-contact and your smile.

9   Find something suitable to wear. You should look smart, clean and tidy, but try to be comfortable.

10   Make sure that you know how to get to the interview venue and that you know how long the journey will take. If you are late owing to unforeseen circumstances, contact the company as soon as possible to apologize and explain why.

CASE STUDY

When we were at school... I do remember vaguely touching upon interviews, but I do think they really need to improve on that 'cos a lot of people don't have the support from home. Some people's parents may never have had a job through no fault of their own, but some people might not know how to do that. I think as part of growing up and learning and in our culture that is an essential thing that the government should try and incorporate in lessons with young people. Because it's a basic skill isn't it, you know, some people just don't know how to behave. I think I did some interview training when I was at sixth form... but that's more for university so it was kind of like when you go to university this is how you should dress. But they should have it for all places of work, whether it's going out for a job, an apprenticeship or university or a standard interview, anything like that there should be a procedure in place I think.

SOURCE Laura, business and administration apprentice, Weymouth

Attending an interview or assessment

When attending an interview, you should take note of the following points:

- Arrive in good time as this will help you to remain calm.
- Smile and shake hands if offered. Maintain good eye-contact.
- Sit only when invited to do so.
- Sit upright, don's slouch and don't fidget. Maintain good eye-contact with everyone in the room, especially the person who is asking the question.

- Listen attentively and don't interrupt when someone else is speaking.
- Speak clearly and confidently.
- Keep to the point. Try not to waffle. If you really don't know an answer, say so.
- Be polite, honest and enthusiastic.

Improving your chances of success

Employers tend to look for the following traits, skills and experiences, so if you can demonstrate as many of these as possible on your application form and during your interview, you are likely to be more successful in obtaining the apprenticeship. Remember that you need to be able to demonstrate how you have gained these abilities: employers will not be impressed if you just reproduce a list with no evidence to back it up. Also, make sure that you demonstrate skills and attributes that are relevant to the position for which you are applying:

- enthusiasm;
- creativity;
- commitment;
- problem solving;
- motivation;
- imagination;
- confidence;
- planning skills;
- team working;
- organizational skills;
- communication skills (written and verbal);
- autonomy;
- numerical skills;
- goal setting;
- initiative;
- sticking to rules and procedures;
- people skills;

- listening to authority;
- empathy;
- quick thinking;
- listening skills;
- working under stress;
- leadership;
- optimism/positivity;
- flexibility;
- honesty;
- diplomacy;
- sociability;
- negotiation skills;
- adaptability;
- analytical skills;
- reflexivity.

Summary

When applying for an apprenticeship it is important to make sure that everything you produce is neatly presented and free from error. This is the case for all types of application, including online forms, paper forms and when producing a CV and covering letter. You need to sell yourself, demonstrating that you would be a valuable asset to the company, and that you have the necessary skills, experience and attributes to succeed.

If you find that you succeed in the application and interview, and you are offered a place on the apprenticeship programme, you need to know more about what it will be like working as apprentice. These issues are discussed in the following chapter.

Further reading

Yate, MJ (2008) *Great Answers to Tough Interview Questions*, Kogan Page, London

Chapter Eight
Working as
an apprentice

If you are successful in your application and you obtain a position on an apprenticeship programme, it is useful to understand more about what working as an apprentice entails. There are basic rights that all employees have and you need to understand these so that you can make sure that they are being met. Also, it is important to know how to balance work and training, improve your ability to work with other employees and apprentices, manage your money, remain motivated and develop and record your transferable skills. These issues are discussed in this chapter.

Understanding your rights

Chapter 3 discusses apprentice work contracts, including information about working hours, sick pay, maternity leave and salaries. It also provides information about implied terms, which are based on custom, practice and agreement reached with trade unions and staff associations. This includes employer and apprenticeship responsibilities such as a duty of trust and a duty to obey. In addition to the rights and responsibilities laid out in the contract, there are other rights that all workers have that are relevant to you as an apprentice. These are discussed below.

Working hours

Child workers

If you are under the mandatory school leaving age (currently 16 and under) you are classed as a child worker and cannot work more than 12 hours a week during term-time. During school holidays 13- to 14-year-olds may work a maximum of 25 hours per week and 15- to 16-year-olds may work a maximum of 35 hours per week. No child worker can work for more than two hours on a Sunday.

Young workers

If you are over school leaving age, but under the age of 18, you may not normally work more than 8 hours a day or 40 hours a week. These hours cannot be averaged out for young workers. In certain circumstances, such as in response to a surge in demand for your service or product, you may be able to work longer hours. However, this can only take place if there is no adult available to take over and if your training needs are not adversely affected. Your employer cannot ask you to work over this limit and, if they do, you can contact the Pay and Work Rights helpline for guidance (see below).

Adult workers

If you are 18 or over you cannot be forced to work more than 48 hours a week on average – this is normally averaged over 17 weeks. You can work more than 48 hours in one week, as long as the average over 17 weeks is less than 48 hours per week. It is possible to opt out of this rule if you wish, but this choice must be voluntary and you must opt out in writing to your employer. Your employer cannot force you to opt out of this rule or force you to work more than 48 hours a week on average.

Annual leave

If you work full-time you are entitled to a minimum of 5.6 weeks paid annual leave (28 days for someone working five days a week). If you work part-time you are entitled to the same level of holiday pro rata (so 5.6 times your usual working week, eg 22.4 days for someone working four days a week). These hours are your minimum entitlement and some employers may offer you more than this. If so, this will be described in your contract. You start to build up your holiday entitlement as soon as you start work with your employer.

You should note, however, that bank and public holidays can be included in your holiday entitlement (there are eight permanent bank and public holidays in England and Wales, nine in Scotland and ten in Northern Ireland). Also, your employer can control when you take your holidays. You will need to give your employer advance notice that you want to take your holiday entitlement. This notice should be at least twice as long as the amount of holiday you want to take. For example, you should give two weeks' notice for one week's holiday. Your employer has to give the same advance notice if they want you to take a holiday at a certain time, such as Christmas or Easter. Some will include this information in your contract of employment.

Sick pay

If you are working for an employer under a contract of service and you are earning at least £102 a week (2011/12 figures), you are entitled to Statutory Sick Pay (SSP) if you are sick for at least four days in a row (including weekends and bank holidays and days that you do not normally work).

The standard rate for SSP is £81.60 a week in 2011/12 and it is usually paid on your normal payday in the same way as your normal earnings. SSP is subject to tax and National Insurance contributions in the same way as your wages, although the amount you receive may be below the amount you need to earn before you pay tax and National Insurance. To receive payments you will need to tell your employer that you are sick and may need to provide medical evidence after eight days of sickness. SSP is not affected if you have to go into hospital.

Some companies may offer Company Sick Pay, which could be more generous than SSP. If so, details will be given in your employment contract. This scheme may be referred to as contractual or occupational sick pay. If your company runs this type of scheme it can choose to make sick payments at its own discretion, which means that it can refuse to make a payment if it thinks your absence is unjustified.

Health and safety

Where health and safety are concerned you have certain rights that are given to you by law. These include the following points (your trainer/assessor should visit your workplace to check that health and safety conditions are being met):

- Your employer must control risks to your health and safety, as far as possible.

- You must be provided with personal protective and safety equipment, free of charge. All manuals must be followed and the equipment must be used or worn correctly.

- You are able to stop work and leave your work area without being disciplined if you have any concerns about health and safety.

- You have the right to tell your employer about any health and safety concerns that you have.

- You have the right to get in touch with the Health and Safety Executive (HSE), your local authority or your trainer/assessor if your employer won't listen to your concerns, without being disciplined.

Breaks and rests

You have the right to rest breaks during the working day and to have time off from work during the working week, in addition to the annual paid holiday described above. For workers over the age of 18 this includes:

- a rest of 20 minutes if you are expected to work for more than six hours in one go;

- a break of at least 11 hours between working days;

- either an uninterrupted 24 hours clear of work each week or an uninterrupted 48 hours clear each fortnight.

For workers under the age of 18 this includes:

- a rest of 30 minutes if you are expected to work for more than four and a half hours in one go;

- 12 uninterrupted hours' rest in each 24-hour period in which you work;

- two days off each week.

Balancing training and work

As we have seen in previous chapters, an apprenticeship programme comprises a mix of work and training. To complete the programme successfully you need to be able to organize and manage your work and training, so that both can be undertaken together and neither impinges on the other. One of the benefits of undertaking an apprenticeship is that the training is directly related to your work, so this, along with the following tips, will make it easier when balancing your work and training:

- Draw up a list of non-negotiable activities that you must carry out each week. This will include your regular working hours, all your training and any other essential activities. Once you understand what hours are to be taken up with work and training it is easier to organize other activities around these times.

- Think of the most efficient way to carry out a task or cope with a problem. Many hours can be wasted trying to sort out a computer problem or carry out an unfamiliar task at work, for example. Ask your mentor and/or trainer for guidance when required.

- Do not procrastinate. The definition of 'procrastinate' is to defer, to delay from day to day. Don't put off your work or training. If you are experiencing problems speak to your boss, mentor or trainer. If you have to complete pieces of work for assessment, do so in good time so that you are not put under pressure.

- Set aside some time for private study if you have to do extra work for a training course or assessment. Try to do this at a time that suits the way you like to work. Make sure that partners, friends or family know that you should not be disturbed at this time. Set a clear start and stop time for your study sessions. You will find that you begin to work faster but don't lose any understanding of the material. If you find that you are having problems completing your work, stop and do something else for a while. You will find it easier to approach your work refreshed.

- Recreation and socializing are important for your frame of mind and well-being. Try to keep a good balance between recreation, work and training. But don't let your social life have a detrimental effect on work, for example through drinking too much alcohol and having too many late nights.

- Don't work or study at a time when you should be sleeping. Sleep is essential for your intellectual, emotional and physical health.

Working successfully with others

Some people find it hard to work and mix with other people when they begin a new job, especially if this is their first job or if they have entered an unfamiliar environment. Younger apprentices can find it daunting because they don't know what to expect and because everyone else in the company is older and friendships have already been formed. Attending training sessions can be worrying for people who may have had bad experiences of formal education in the past.

Nervousness in a new apprenticeship is to be expected and you should not worry about this: your nerves will diminish as you become more familiar with your role, the training environment and with other people in the organization. Most people want you to do well and will help as much as possible, both in your work and training.

The key to getting on well with others is to improve your social and communication skills. You can do this by taking note of the following points:

- When talking to other employees, apprentices or your employer, always make eye-contact with them as this shows that you are interested in what they are saying. Try not to be distracted when someone is speaking. Don't fiddle with a pen, look out the window or respond to others who are not speaking. Make sure that you let someone finish speaking: don't jump to conclusions about what they are going to say. Although it is acceptable to interrupt occasionally with a well-thought-out question or opinion, don't do it too often or in a confrontational way as this will cause ill-feeling and may lead to colleagues becoming defensive.

- If you are unsure of what your boss, mentor or trainer is saying, ask questions. Try to ask open questions that start with words such as 'what', 'why', 'where' and 'how' as people cannot answer these with a simple yes or no and will have to elaborate on what they are saying.

- Explain your opinions clearly and concisely. Don't take things personally when people don't agree with your opinions. Be patient: if someone doesn't seem to understand what you are saying, try to explain yourself in a different way. Don't assume that you are right all the time. Be open to other ideas and opinions. However, if you are certain of your views, don't be persuaded by alternative arguments, especially when they are expressed more forcefully than yours. Be confident and assertive, but not rude or aggressive.

- Try to mix with other employees and trainees away from the workplace. This enables you to get to know them better, which will help you to mix better and relax more at work.

Managing your money

Chapter 4 highlighted the importance of making sure that you have enough money to meet your basic needs when you choose an apprenticeship. This includes having enough money for accommodation, fuel, transport, clothing and food. You also need to make sure that you don't spend your hard-earned money too quickly (perhaps because this is the first time you have received a wage). To do this effectively you need to understand how to manage your money and plan your budget. This involves five simple stages:

- Keep all records of your income (eg salary, overtime, travel grants, bank interest).

- Keep all records of your expenditure (eg rent, food bills, utility bills, cash withdrawals).

- Calculate your income.

- Calculate your expenditure.

- Work out the difference between the two.

Today there are a number of useful budget calculators available online to help you to work out your budget (enter 'budget calculator' into your search engine to be directed to relevant sites). If you find that the difference between the two is positive (in the black) you need to try to keep it that way. However, if the difference between the two is negative (in the red) you need to think about what you are going to do to change the balance in your favour. This involves reducing your expenditure and/or increasing your income. This should be done as soon as possible because once you get into debt you could find that this debt increases quickly out of control. Speak to your boss about obtaining overtime, speak to your trainer about obtaining a training grant and/or travel expenses and cut down on your spending, where possible (see quotation below). You could also think about purchasing an NUS Extra card if it will help you to save money (see below).

CASE STUDY

I didn't get a lot of money in my job at first, so it was quite hard to manage on the small amount I had, because in my previous job I was paid more. When I got less it was hard to manage. So I asked my trainer and he sorted some cash for me, some grant or something, so that helped. And I stayed in more nights so that saved some money.

SOURCE Chris, motor vehicle apprentice, Weymouth College

Travel expenses

During the research for this book, I found that one of the main problems encountered by apprentices was the cost of travel, both to work and to the training venue, if it was located elsewhere. Some of the apprentices were not receiving travel expenses and were finding it very hard to meet the costs (see Michael's case study in Appendix 3). If travel expenses are a problem for you, the following points may help:

- When choosing an apprenticeship, ask about travel expenses. Some employers will agree to pay these for you, which could provide significant financial help.

- When choosing a college or training provider, find out about the support they offer to help with travel. Some of this support can help apprentices who are struggling to pay for travel. For example, Weymouth College provides the following services for students:

  - a Travel Centre to help students meet their travel needs;
  - bus or train passes for students living more than five miles from the college (with the opportunity to pay in instalments);
  - coaches, minibuses or dedicated bus services for students living in various parts of Dorset.

- If you are working for your local council, find out whether they offer subsidized travel for apprentices. For example, Bristol City Council announced in March 2010 that apprentices would be eligible for reduced fares on First buses for the duration of their apprenticeship.

- Find out if there is a local charity that will help with travel (your trainer/assessor or local advice centre should be able to offer advice about this; see case study, below).

- If you cannot receive any financial help towards travel, try to cut down on costs, for example look into car sharing (or obtaining a lift from a work colleague, neighbour or friend who is travelling in the same direction). Annual bus and train passes are cheaper and remember to use all young person/student discounts to which you may be entitled.

CASE STUDY

I think you can get a grant for your travel expenses. There's a scheme in Weymouth called the Samuel Mico Trust, have you heard of them? They helped me when I was at my placement... because I literally had no money and I had to buy like pens, books folders, just things like that, and they gave me a grant towards that and I was really appreciative of that. They help with tuition fees, equipment fees and they help all apprentices and young people. I found out about that through Waves [the local youth advice centre], so that was really helpful. They have a limited amount of money so you have to fill out an application form and you have to submit it and it's for their consideration so if you really do need it then they consider you.

SOURCE Laura, business and administration apprentice, Weymouth

NUS Extra Card

The National Union of Students (NUS) provides an 'NUS Extra' card that enables students to obtain discounts on a wide variety of goods and services. Recently, the NUS have extended the eligibility criteria to include students in schools, professional organizations, distance learners and work-based learners (which includes apprentices). In 2011 this card costs £11 for a year and entitles you to a wide variety of discounts and rewards. Visit **www.nus.org.uk/en/NUS-Extra** for more information and to purchase a card. A value calculator is available on this site to show you how much you could save. If you are on a low wage as an apprentice, you may find that purchasing this card helps you to spend less.

Remaining motivated

As we saw in Chapter 6, the easiest way to remain motivated is to make sure that you choose an apprenticeship programme in which you have a high level of interest. Also, you will find it easier to remain enthusiastic if you are interested in your training and you get on with other people within the organization for which you work.

However, you may find that the apprenticeship programme does not turn out as you expected and that your motivation levels begin to fall. This could be for a number of reasons, including:

- the training and/or work is not providing you with enough stimulation;
- you are not being given the chance to develop your skills, knowledge and experience;
- you are finding the whole programme boring;
- you do not get on with the other employees and/or apprentices;
- your boss/mentor is not helping and supporting you;
- you are not happy with the working conditions.

If you are experiencing any of these problems you need to talk to your boss, mentor or trainer. Talk to the person whom you find the easiest to approach as they might be able to raise the issues with others on your behalf. If you are finding the work/training boring, or you are not being stimulated enough, your boss might be able to allocate more complex or more interesting tasks. Also, your trainer might be able to provide you with more stimulating training that helps to get you motivated.

If you are really unhappy with your employer and you are unable to resolve the issues, yet you are enjoying your apprenticeship, it may be possible to change your employer and remain on your apprenticeship programme. Speak to your training adviser to find out whether this is possible and to ascertain whether they know of another suitable employer who could take you on.

Developing transferable skills

You will find it easier to remain motivated and go on to complete your apprenticeship successfully if you are able to understand and keep a record of the transferable skills that you are developing. These are skills that you develop while you are working and studying (and during life in general) that can be transferred easily to the world of work. They will help you to obtain employment and promotion in the future.

Prospective employers are keen to see that you have developed, and are aware of, such skills. They are not interested solely in the competencies that you have gained from your training, but are interested also in any skills and attributes that will help you to carry out your job effectively and make you a valuable member of the workforce.

Examples of skills that you could develop during the term of your apprenticeship include:

- communication skills (verbal and written);
- listening skills;
- social skills;
- the ability to empathize with/support others:
- adaptability and flexibility;
- independent work/study skills;
- organization skills;
- time management;
- the ability to meet deadlines/set goals;
- the ability to work under pressure;
- crisis management;
- skills of reflection;
- problem-solving skills;
- skills of analysis, evaluation and synthesis;
- reviewing and critiquing skills;
- IT skills;
- numerical skills;
- reading skills;
- team-working skills.

Keep a diary (paper or electronic) during the term of your apprenticeship as this is the best way to recognize and record the skills that you are developing as the programme progresses. It will be a useful source of information when you need to provide details of your skills on job application forms in the future.

CASE STUDY

In Spring 2011 the Student Loans Company (SLC) took on 13 apprentices in customer service and administration. The apprentices are based in Darlington and are working towards an NVQ Level 2 in business administration through Darlington College. The SLC is looking to expand its apprenticeship programme in Darlington and also roll out the programme in Glasgow. For more information about the SLC, visit **www.slc.co.uk** and for more information about Darlington College, visit **www.darlington.ac.uk**.

Summary

All employees have certain rights, which include the right to holiday, rest breaks and sick pay. If you feel these rights are not being met you should raise the issue first with your employer or trainer. As an apprentice, it is important that you are able to balance your work and training, get on well with employees and apprentices, manage your money, remain motivated and improve your skills as the programme progresses. This will help you to obtain employment and promotion in the future.

Once you have completed your apprenticeship programme there are various routes open to you, including full-time employment and further learning at college or university. These issues are discussed in the following chapter.

Further information

More information about pay and work rights can be obtained from:

Pay and Work Rights Helpline: 0800 917 2368
Website: **http://payandworkrightscampaign.direct.gov.uk**

www.horsesmouth.co.uk
This website provides a social network for informal mentoring. The NAS has formed a partnership with Horsesmouth 'to encourage people who have been through an apprenticeship to mentor and inspire others in a safe and friendly social online environment'. Visit this site to find apprenticeship mentors and for information about what an apprenticeship entails from those who have completed a similar programme.

Chapter Nine
Progressing on from an apprenticeship

Once you have completed your apprenticeship successfully there are various options available to you. These include obtaining full-time employment or moving on to a higher-level apprenticeship with your current employer, moving on to another job with a different employer, accessing various learning and earning schemes and going on to full-time study at university or college. These progression routes are discussed in this chapter.

Staying with the same employer

In general there are two options available if you wish to stay with your current employer: moving on to a higher-level apprenticeship or obtaining a full-time position with your employer.

Moving on to a higher-level apprenticeship

Some companies provide the opportunity to start a lower-level apprenticeship, for example a Level 2 apprenticeship in England, and then move on to a higher-level apprenticeship (Level 3 in England) once the first programme has been completed successfully (see case study, below). However, not all organizations offer this option so if it is something that interests you it is important to look into the availability of this type of progression before you make your initial application. Also, to be offered a place at a higher level, you will have to demonstrate enthusiasm, commitment and loyalty to the company, along with the successful completion of the first apprenticeship programme.

CASE STUDY

Boots Opticians offers Apprenticeship and Advanced Apprenticeship programmes that start with a four-week induction programme to welcome staff to Boots Opticians and help them get to know the branch environment. On the Apprenticeship programme apprentices work towards an NVQ Level 2 in Optical Retailing and undertake Key Skills training, supported throughout by a personal 'buddy' and the branch manager. The programme includes seven days' training at the Boots custom-built training centre.

Once the Level 2 apprenticeship has been completed and apprentices have gained optical consulting experience, they have the opportunity to achieve an NVQ Level 3 (the Advanced Apprenticeship) and become a senior optical consultant. This takes around 18 months and the skills gained enable apprentices to earn around 30 per cent more than when they joined Boots Opticians at the beginning of the programme. For more information about this scheme, visit **www.boots.jobs/opticians**.

As we can see from Laura's case study in Appendix 3, it is also possible to work with your employer and local training provider to develop a personal progression route that involves both a higher-level apprenticeship and additional professional qualifications. This will only be possible if you have developed a good working relationship with your employer and they are happy for you to continue your training within the organization.

Obtaining a full-time position

Although an employer is not obliged to provide a job for you at the end of your apprenticeship programme, many apprentices are offered a full-time position if they have completed the programme successfully and are a valuable member of the workforce. Many of the larger employers have a clear progression structure, which takes apprentices through the various levels of apprenticeship and on to other types of training, qualifications and higher-level positions within the company (see case study below).

CASE STUDY

Scottish and Southern Energy has an apprenticeship programme that enables apprentices to progress within the company. Indeed, many of the existing senior managers and directors started work as apprentices with the company. For example, a possible progression route involves work as an apprentice engineer, moving on to a trainee engineer, on to a qualified engineer and then on to the Manager Development Programme. For more information about apprenticeship programmes and progression routes with Scottish and Southern Electric, visit **www.sse-apprentices.co.uk**.

Moving on to another job

Some companies may be unable to offer a full-time position within their organization after you have completed the apprenticeship, and this may be especially so during times of economic uncertainty. In other cases you may decide that you wish to move on to another organization, even if you are offered a full-time position at the end of your apprenticeship programme. This could be because you feel it would help your career if you changed employers, or perhaps you have decided that you would prefer to work for another company because it offers more opportunities or more of a challenge (see case study below).

CASE STUDY

I did enjoy my apprenticeship but I didn't want to stay there any more. It was a small dealership and they'd been good to me, but even my boss told me to try the Ford dealership. He said there would be more chances for me there. So I applied and got the job. Now I work for myself and I'm looking for a new garage because I need the space. It was good to get the experience with Ford. Maybe I'll have my own apprentice one day but insurance might stop me.

SOURCE Clive, motor mechanic, Northamptonshire

If you decide that you wish to move on to another company, your chances of success will be greatly improved if you are able to do well on your apprenticeship programme, have a good attendance record and have shown that you are keen to succeed in both your work and training. You will need to ask your current employer for a reference, and this will be more positive if you have been a valuable member of the workforce and if your employer has been pleased with your progress.

Making a job application

Often you will find it easier to apply for another job when you are already in employment. This is because it takes the urgency out of your application: you can take the time to choose a job that interests you and you aren't pressured financially into rushing your application. Also, some future employers are likely to look more favourably on people who are already in employment because it shows that you have work experience and are able to meet all the required work commitments. Therefore, you should apply for other jobs before your apprenticeship programme ends, or you should take a full-time position if it is offered and then apply for other positions at a later date and without the need for too much urgency.

When applying for other jobs, take notice of the application and interview advice offered in Chapters 7 and 15. Also, you may find it useful to seek advice from a professional careers adviser. Contact details are provided in Chapter 4.

Accessing learning and earning schemes

Apprenticeships are learning and earning schemes because they offer you the chance to train and learn new skills while working and receiving a wage. If learning and earning schemes interest you, there are other schemes that you may like to consider after your current programme (see Chapter 5 and Further Reading, below). It may also be possible to convince your employer to support you through an FE or HE course by providing time off for study and through helping you to meet the costs of the course (see Laura's case study in Appendix 3).

If this is a route that interests you, speak to your employer and/or trainer to find out what options are available. Again, you will find that you are more successful in convincing your employer if you have done very well on your apprenticeship programme and have become a valuable member of the workforce.

CASE STUDY

Balfour Beatty offers the following learning and earning opportunities:

- apprenticeships in electrical, mechanical or plumbing services engineering, construction trades and highways maintenance;

- technician traineeships leading to National and Higher National Certificate and Diploma qualifications in civil and railway engineering, electrical/mechanical services engineering and building;

- trainee quantity surveyors and contract administrators;

- part-time degree study in construction, engineering and quantity surveying disciplines.

These positions are available throughout the UK. For more information, visit **www.balfourbeatty.com**.

Moving on to college or university

Another progression route that is available after the successful completion of an apprenticeship programme is to move on to college or university to study full-time. Indeed, the Coalition government has expressed an interest in encouraging a closer relationship between further and higher education, opening up routes for people who wish to progress from vocational programmes.

John Hayes, Minister for Further Education, said at the Association of Colleges conference in Birmingham in November 2010 that apprenticeships should become a route to higher learning, and that more HE qualifications (other than degrees) should be developed to encourage people to take this route. The government has also announced its intention to introduce a student loans-style system to provide funds for people studying for Level 3 qualifications who are over the age of 24.

Applying to university

Advanced and higher apprenticeship frameworks will be considered for UCAS Tariff points for Level 3 and Level 4 qualifications within the Qualification and Credits Framework (QCF) from April 2011. This means that the qualifications that you receive on your apprenticeship programme can be used in your application to university. (UCAS stands for Universities and Colleges Admissions Service, which is the organization that is responsible for managing applications to almost all full-time undergraduate degree programmes at UK universities and colleges. UCAS Tariff is the points system used by universities to assess the qualifications held by applicants when deciding whether they should be offered a place at university.) For more information about UCAS, visit **www.ucas.ac.uk** and for more information about the QCF, visit **www.ofqual.gov.uk**.

Working out the costs

From 2012 universities will be able to charge up to £9,000 a year for undergraduate degree courses (this is for tuition fees and does not include accommodation, which can cost an additional £2,500–3,000 a year, at current levels). Students do not have to pay fees up front, but instead will be able to take out a student loan to cover the cost of fees. Once students have finished university they will begin to repay their loans when their earnings are over £21,000 a year, up from £15,000 under the current system (while their earnings are under £21,000, no loan repayments are required). Student loans are also available for maintenance and will be repaid in the same way.

Students from lower-income families will be able to benefit from a new £150 million National Scholarships Programme, which will help to reduce loan debt by providing free foundation courses or one-year bursaries, for example. Universities may also offer bursaries for students from low-income families and a maintenance grant of up to £3,250 will be available for students with a household income of less than £25,000. For more detailed information about paying for university, see Further reading, below.

CASE STUDY

Some of my engineering mates went to university, but I thought I can't afford it, so I decided not to go. I would have liked to and I think I would have done well but it was just too expensive. And the course was four years long. So when I finished my apprenticeship I carried on working with the same company rather than go to university. I might do a part-time course later because I do like the study, but only if I can afford to, which will probably be never with the way things are going.

SOURCE Louise, engineering apprentice, 2008–10, Bournemouth

Seeking advice and guidance

The importance of seeking professional careers advice and guidance was stressed in Chapter 4. If you are in any doubt about how you wish your career to progress you should obtain this type of professional advice. See Chapters 4 and 13 for contact details of organizations offering advice. Also, if you are thinking about taking part in further or higher education, or other learning and earning schemes, you may find it useful to visit some of the websites listed below for more information:

- **www.studentfinanceengland.co.uk**: this website will direct you to all the information that you require about financial support for higher education in England.

- **www.studentfinancewales.co.uk**: if you are a Welsh student more information about student finance for further and higher education in Wales can be obtained from this website.

- **www.saas.gov.uk**: if you are a Scottish student more information about student finance, including application forms and procedures, can be obtained from this site.

- **www.studentfinanceni.co.uk**: you can find out all the information you need about funding for students from Northern Ireland on this website.

- **www.ucas.ac.uk**: UCAS is the organization responsible for managing applications to HE courses in the UK. On this website you can find all the information you need about applying for higher education and there is a useful student budget calculator available.

- **www.scholarship-search.org.uk**: this website provides a comprehensive guide to student finance and has been developed by Hot Courses in association with UCAS. There is a useful budget planner and funding database available on this site.

- **www.hotcourses.com**: this website provides comprehensive and up-to-date information about all universities in the UK, containing useful reviews to help you with your course and university choice.

- **www.push.co.uk**: you can read university profiles on this website. Universities are rated in the following categories: academic, sports, activities, housing, welfare, reputation and living costs. You can also find out about leisure and entertainment, along with up-to-date prices of alcoholic drinks at each university.

- **www.prospects.ac.uk:** Prospects is an organization that provides advice and guidance to university students and graduates about careers, work experience and study abroad.

- **www.direct.gov.uk:** visit the education and learning section of this government information site for more information about all aspects of education and learning, including learning and earning schemes, student finance and making career choices.

- **http://unistats.direct.gov.uk:** Unistats is a government website that contains statistics about universities in the UK, some of which are based on the results of the National Student Survey. Visit this site if you want to find out how universities compare with each other on criteria such as student satisfaction and employment prospects.

Summary

If you find that you have enjoyed the training aspect of your apprenticeship programme you could consider moving on to other learning and earning schemes, a higher-level apprenticeship or going on to study full-time at college or university. Your apprenticeship qualifications will be recognized in your application for college and university if you intend to take this route. Other apprentices find that they prefer to move on to full-time employment, and this may be possible with your current employer or you can decide to move on to another employer. If you are in any doubt about how you wish your career to progress, you should seek professional advice and guidance.

This section of the book has provided information for school leavers, students and adult learners who are interested in apprenticeship schemes. The next section goes on to offer advice for parents, beginning with a discussion that helps parents to decide whether an apprenticeship is the most appropriate route for their child.

Further reading

Dawson, C (2010) *Learn While You Earn: Everything you need to know about learning new skills while still earning money*, Kogan Page, London

Dawson, C (2009) *The Essential Guide to Paying for University: Effective funding strategies for parents and students*, Kogan Page, London

Part Three
Information for parents

Chapter Ten
Is an apprenticeship right for your children?

My research for this book suggests that parents have not heard a great deal about the modern-day apprenticeship programmes that are available and that they are unsure about whether the apprenticeship route is a viable option for their children. If you are a parent and you are interested in finding out more, this chapter helps you to understand the facts, overcome misconceptions and assess your children's wants and needs. It also helps you to know about the skills that can be gained, look at possible alternative routes for your children, assess the advantages and disadvantages and help your children to seek professional advice and guidance.

Understanding the facts

Apprenticeships provide the opportunity for your children to train on the job alongside experienced workers/mentors. Apprentices receive a wage while they are working and training, which must be at least £2.60 an hour. They may also receive additional money for essential books, clothing or equipment, or to help them with a disability. As an apprentice, they will receive the same benefits as other employees such as pension contributions, leisure facilities and subsidized canteen meals. Some of the larger companies offer additional perks such as overseas travel, clothing and company entertainment.

Training can take place in the workplace or at a dedicated training centre or college and can be on a day release or block release basis. Qualifications are nationally recognized and provide the opportunity for your children to advance in their chosen career sector. Apprentices are monitored at various stages to make sure that they are progressing and meeting their targets.

Apprenticeships are based on frameworks that are devised by SSCs, which are state-sponsored, employer-led organizations that cover specific economic sectors in the UK (see Chapter 1). If your children undertake an apprenticeship, they will work towards the following:

- A knowledge-based certificate such as a Technical Certificate, BTEC or City & Guilds qualification.

- A competence-based certificate such as an NVQ or SVQ.

- A Functional Skills Certificate. This includes practical skills in English, information and communication technology and mathematics.

- Other qualifications, requirements or certificates as specified by the particular occupation.

Your children will also need to develop an understanding of Employer Rights and Responsibilities, including issues such as health and safety and equal opportunities, and develop their personal learning and thinking skills (evidence of these must be demonstrated, perhaps through a workbook or by attaining specific qualifications, for example).

Apprenticeships can take between one and four years to complete depending on the level of apprenticeship, the apprentices' ability and the industry sector. Apprentices have a special form of employment contract: in essence it is a contract for training, rather than for employment. However, all apprenticeships are also covered by relevant employment legislation, which includes issues such as working hours, holiday entitlement and levels of pay. More information about apprenticeship employment contracts and working conditions is provided in Chapter 3 and more information about working as an apprentice is provided in Chapter 8.

CASE STUDY

Access is a training company based in Gateshead that operates throughout the North East region. It is a provider of apprenticeship programmes, offering Apprenticeships at Level 2, Advanced Apprenticeships at Level 3 and Higher Apprenticeships at Level 4 in the following sectors:

- Business Administration (Levels 2 and 3);

- Accounting (Levels 2, 3 and 4);

- Team Leading and Management (Levels 2 and 3);

- Customer Service (Levels 2 and 3);

- Teaching and Learning (Level 3);

- Manufacturing Operations (Level 2);

- Security Systems Engineering (Level 3);

- Warehousing and Distribution (Levels 2 and 3).

These apprenticeships are available for anyone over the age of 16, and are 'aimed at those starting a career, looking to progress to higher levels, or for those with experience but without the formal qualifications to support that experience'. They are available for people who are already in employment or for those who are looking for work. Access is able to match suitable candidates with suitable employers. For more information about Access and their apprenticeship programme, visit **www.accesstraining.org.uk**.

Overcoming misconceptions

CASE STUDY

I must admit I think of apprenticeships like they were when I was young. You worked for a company for life. They trained you and you stayed with them. I know those days are gone now though because nobody seems to stay with a company for very long and it's all so precarious, what with the economy in the state it's in. I just do worry for my children. What prospects are there for young people today? So I'm interested to find out more about these new apprenticeships, but I really don't know much about them. Nobody seems to tell you much do they?

SOURCE Annette, parent of 14-year-old twins, Weymouth

As we can see from the quotation above, there is some confusion surrounding the modern-day apprenticeship scheme. During my research for this book parents said that they were confused about the scheme and were unsure of what was being offered to young people. Some also displayed scepticism, believing that the programme was a 'government ploy to fix unemployment figures' or that employers would 'take on apprentices to get government money and then sack them as soon as the money ran out'.

This book should help to address some of this confusion. If you are a parent who is thinking that an apprenticeship might be a suitable route for your children, read the first section of the book as it provides information about the history and structure of apprenticeships, along with details about how the scheme works. You should note also that although young trainees may be referred to as 'apprentices' (and have been throughout history: see Chapter 1), this book refers to those who are employed on a 'contract of apprenticeship' and those on a publicly funded apprenticeship programme (see Chapter 2 for a description of these programmes). It may be possible for an employer to offer an apprenticeship place that is outside this scheme, so you will need to check what type of scheme is being offered to your children before they sign any contract or agreement with an employer.

Assessing your children's wants, needs and skills

As parents you may feel that you know what is best for your children. This can tempt you to push them into a career that they might not enjoy. Other parents try to live their lives through their children, perhaps persuading their offspring to go to university because they didn't have the chance to go to university themselves. University is not something that all people enjoy, and if your children are persuaded to go when they really don't want to, it is possible that they could have an unfulfilling experience, will not be motivated and could drop out. Employers look unfavourably on prospective candidates who have dropped out of university, so this type of persuasiveness could be detrimental to your children's chances in the future.

However, most parents want what is best for their children and are very good at helping them to think about what they want in the future. Despite this, there are some teenagers who are not enthusiastic about discussing their future, having no idea what they want to do, or indeed whether they actually want to do anything. As parents, therefore, you may need to help your children to assess their wants and needs. Chapter 4 provides information about how your children can begin to think about these issues, and provides information about undertaking a self-evaluation. Chapter 6 takes this further by providing a choices checklist. Work through these sections with your children, helping them to overcome any barriers or problems. If you are still no closer to helping your children to reach conclusions about their future direction, you may find it useful to seek professional advice and guidance (see below).

CASE STUDY

Forget university; that simply shows you how to find information and assimilate facts. An apprenticeship will teach you skills and how to use them and it is skill that puts dinner on the table.

SOURCE Ian Brooke, Weymouth, apprentice 1958–63, via e-mail

Knowing about the skills that can be gained

As we saw in Chapter 1, SSCs are licensed by government to work with employers to develop National Occupational Standards and design apprenticeship frameworks for the industries they represent. At this present time, 23 SSCs represent over 90 per cent of the workforce.

All apprenticeship frameworks in England can be viewed by using the 'framework search', available in the 'partners' section on the NAS website (**www.apprenticeships.org.uk**). This search facility contains an alphabetical listing of all frameworks by title (such as 'accountancy', 'beauty therapy' and 'cabin crew'), a list of the NVQ level available and the SSC that has developed the framework. You can use this search facility to find out more about the skills and competencies that your child can develop on a specific apprenticeship programme. A similar list for Scotland can be obtained from **www.skillsdevelopmentscotland.co.uk**.

In addition to the skills and competences outlined in the frameworks, your child should be able to gain other valuable skills, such as working well in a team, organization skills and social skills. For a comprehensive list of the transferable skills that could be gained by undertaking an apprenticeship programme, see Chapter 8.

CASE STUDY

In 2009/10, almost 20,000 people in Scotland started a Modern Apprenticeship programme, enabling them to gain the skills, training and experience required for successful long-term employment. This figure exceeded the target of 18,500 and, according to Alex Salmond, Scotland's First Minister, this is impressive in times of 'severe economic turbulence' and 'tight public expenditure due to the £500 million Westminster cuts'. For more information about apprenticeships in Scotland, visit **www.skillsdevelopmentscotland.co.uk**.

Understanding the alternatives

There are various alternative career progression routes available to your children. These include:

- Enrolling on a further education course. Options could include NVQs, BTECs, A levels, City & Guilds qualifications, for example, and study could be full- or part-time. Courses can be vocational, academic or a mixture of both. More information about British qualifications is provided in Chapter 14.

- Enrolling on a higher education course. Options could include foundation degrees or Bachelor degrees, for example, and could include full-time or part-time study. Foundation degrees tend to be the more vocational option, although it is possible to study for a Bachelor degree that includes an element of work experience. More information about these degrees is provided in Chapter 14.

- Learning and earning opportunities. This could include government training schemes that provide the opportunity to train while earning a wage, or schemes that offer university study while your children are working (see Chapter 5).

- Obtaining full-time employment.

- Taking a gap year. Some young people are unsure about their future direction, and taking a gap year, in which they undertake paid employment or voluntary work, enables them to think more about whether they would like to return to education or move into full-time paid employment after their gap year.

Chapter 5 describes the various routes that are available for your child in detail. You may also find it useful to consult the Further reading section in Chapter 9 for more information about the type of schemes that are available.

Assessing the advantages and disadvantages

When thinking about the advantages and disadvantages that your children could experience through taking part in an apprenticeship programme, you need to recognize that the issue is highly subjective. For example, all organizations involved in the delivery of apprenticeships, such as the government, SSCs, professional bodies, learning providers and specific employers, are requested to adhere to 'the apprenticeship brand identity'. As such, the information provided may follow specific guidelines and styles that can stifle independence and impartiality. You need to be able to see through this brand identity when assessing the advantages and disadvantages for your child.

In addition to this, the NAS has various statistics available to convince employers and parents that apprenticeships are a good route to take. You need to read all such information with a critical mind. Who has provided the information? Why have they provided the information? What evidence is available to back up assertions or enable you to verify the accuracy of statistics? Have you considered alternative sources of information that has been provided by organizations and people who do not have a vested interest in the programme?

Questioning the information in this way will help you to think more about the advantages and disadvantages. In addition to this you need to consider apprenticeships together with alternative progression routes. For example, while some young people may believe that £2.60 an hour is not much of a wage, when this is considered alongside a possible debt of at least £35,000 after three years of university study, the small wage perhaps doesn't seem so small (university tuition fees are to rise to up to £9,000 a year from 2012). However, if your children were to take a full-time job with a higher wage, £2.60 an hour does not seem very much. But then, would your children receive any training and the opportunity to obtain further qualifications (which could boost their income in the future) if they were to obtain a full-time job? And how would their full-time wage compare with the higher wages that they could receive as their apprenticeship programme progresses?

Perceived advantages and disadvantages

During my research for this book, apprentices, parents, employers and guidance workers were asked to list perceived advantages and disadvantages. As you will see from the following lists, these are subjective and may vary, depending on individual and family circumstances. Also, you will see that one person's advantage may be another person's disadvantage, so you need to think about each programme in relation to you and your child's circumstances.

Possible advantages:

- Apprentices get the opportunity to train on the job.
- Apprentices receive a wage from day one.
- Apprentices may be entitled to other benefits, such as gym membership, a pension scheme and subsidized canteen facilities.
- Apprentices work with experienced workers who can provide mentoring facilities and support.
- Apprentices get to meet other trainees/apprentices when they are training.
- Most colleges/training organizations provide an excellent level of training.
- Colleges/training providers carry out a health and safety assessment of the workplace to ensure that an apprentice's working environment is safe.
- College staff/trainers can keep employers in check, filtering out 'bad' or unscrupulous employers.
- The company may offer a job at the end of the programme.
- It is cheaper than going to university.
- Apprentices get work experience that they probably won't get if they go to university.
- Employers prefer people to have work experience and qualifications, rather than one or the other.

Possible disadvantages:

- £2.60 is a very small wage.
- Some companies don't offer any extra perks or benefits.
- Young apprentices can find it difficult to juggle work and training, especially if it is their first full-time position since leaving school.

- Young apprentices find it difficult to mix in some working environments, especially if there is an older, well-established workforce.

- Some employers don't take the commitment seriously and fail to provide adequate training or support.

- Unscrupulous employers can exploit vulnerable trainees.

- Some employers are unwilling to offer a job at the end of the programme, instead preferring to employ another apprentice because they can receive money for training and can pay a lower wage.

- Apprentices find that the programme is not what they expected.

- Higher-level qualifications can be gained at university, and employers look more favourably on candidates who have got degrees.

Seeking advice and guidance

The list above shows that, if your children decide to embark on an apprenticeship programme, problems can be encountered. Some of these are because apprentices have not carried out enough research or sought sufficient advice and guidance. Therefore, it is important to encourage your children to find out all they can about their career progression, and, if they decide that they wish to pursue an apprenticeship, it is imperative that they find out all they can about the programme and their prospective employer (Chapter 6 offers advice about how to do this). Through careful research, your children should be able to overcome some of the problems outlined above.

Chapter 4 offers advice about seeking advice and guidance. If your child is unconfident or nervous, it is possible to visit guidance workers with your child. However, guidance workers will not take too kindly to pushy parents who believe that they know what's best for their children (even if you do!). Let your children speak and discuss what is important to them so that the guidance worker can offer the best advice suited to your children's needs.

If your children would like to follow the apprenticeship route, try to encourage them to speak to other apprentices, as this will provide practical information and advice from people who have been through the scheme. They can do this by visiting **www.horsesmouth.co.uk**. This website provides a social network for informal mentoring and has been formed in partnership with the NAS 'to encourage people who have been through an apprenticeship to mentor and inspire others in a safe and friendly social online environment'.

CASE STUDY

The Institute of Leadership and Management (ILM) is the professional body for leaders and managers. Recently, it has developed new management apprenticeship packages that offer a comprehensive development route for new and aspiring managers by combining essential management theory with hands-on practical skills and experience. ILM apprenticeships are available in Team Leading at Level 2 and in Management at Level 3. For more information, visit **www.i-l-m.com**.

Summary

This chapter is aimed at parents and provides further information about apprenticeship programmes to help you to work out whether an apprenticeship is an appropriate route for your children. It is important that you understand what an apprenticeship entails and know how your children will benefit through taking part in such a programme. It is also important to think about the alternative career routes so that you can weigh up the advantages and disadvantages for your children.

Once you have understood more about apprenticeships you can go on to offer advice to your children and help them to make sensible decisions and career choices. These issues are discussed in the next chapter.

Chapter Eleven
Helping with decision making

Now that you understand more about what an apprenticeship pro-gramme entails, and you think it could offer a potential career progression route for your children, it is important to think about how you can help with their decision making. To do this successfully you need to know how to find and present information about all the alternatives, discuss the pros and cons of each option, encourage effective decisions and reach consensus while avoiding arguments. These issues are discussed in this chapter.

Presenting unbiased information to your children

'Bias' is a term that is used to describe a tendency or a preference for a par-ticular line of thought, idea, perspective or result. As we saw in the previous chapter, there is a temptation for some parents to become a little too pushy when discussing their children's future career route (usually because they feel that they know what is best for their children). This can encourage par-ents to present biased information to their children, or encourage others to do so, as the following quotation demonstrates.

CASE STUDY

I once had a parent come with the client and my goodness, he just didn't shut up. Actually the client was over 18 so I was a little surprised that the parent was there at all... But I don't know, I just got the impression the client wasn't able to talk about what they really wanted. But what do you do in that situation? I kept addressing the questions to the client, but the dad would answer every time. But the client gave their consent for the dad to be there so what could I do? The dad was set on university even if it wasn't the best option for the client... he wanted only information about universities but I felt it was important to discuss other options as well, you know, in an unbiased way.

SOURCE Advice worker who wishes to remain anonymous, from South West England

Luckily, most parents are more sensible than this, wanting to present the information in an unbiased way so that their children can make their own informed choices. When doing so it may be helpful to consider the following points:

- Try to conduct as much research as possible about all the alternatives. Search the internet and speak to employers, parents, apprentices and students. Chapter 5 provides more information about the options that are available but it may be helpful to gain some personal accounts from people known to you and your children.

- Recognize the difference between statistics, facts, arguments and opinions (see Chapter 6). You also need to know how to critique and analyse the sources of information that you find to help you make judgements about the validity and reliability of information you are presenting to your children. Encourage your children to do the same when searching for their own information.

- When compiling information to present to your children, try not to be affected by your personal opinions about what is best for your offspring. If you do, this will make you favour certain progression routes above others and may encourage you to miss out certain programmes or routes.

- Try to avoid jargon and technical terms, avoid emotive information (such as highly subjective accounts of good and bad progression routes, for example), present information in a clear and unambiguous way and make sure that you don't overload your children with too much information.

However, if you feel that you haven't got the time or expertise to conduct the necessary research, or you feel that you are unable to present unbiased information, you should think about helping your children to seek professional advice and guidance. More information about this is provided in Chapter 10.

Discussing the pros and cons

As we saw in Chapter 10, there are many advantages and disadvantages associated with following the apprenticeship route, and these depend on your family circumstances and the wants and needs of your children. This is also the case with other types of progression route, such as studying full-time at college or university or obtaining full-time employment.

When discussing the pros and cons, again, you need to gather all the information that you can and discuss the issues in an unbiased way, helping your children to consider the advantages and disadvantages for themselves. Issues that you may need to discuss include personal, financial and career pros and cons.

Personal pros and cons

It is important to choose a career progression route that will help your children to grow in personal confidence and self-esteem. My research has shown that people who have higher levels of confidence and self-esteem believe that they have more choices available in life. They tend to be more confident in trying new jobs and putting themselves forward for promotion and requesting higher salaries. These people tend to be more successful owing to their high levels of confidence, often getting what they want. This is because people perceive them to be confident 'go-getters' who will be an asset in the workforce.

However, greater confidence and self-esteem is not all about succeeding in the world of employment. It is also about feeling satisfied, fulfilled and happy with life. People with higher levels of confidence and self-esteem tend to travel more often, socialize to a greater degree and have more stable relationships.

Therefore you have to take the time to work out together which route is best for your children. While university is perfect for some, it is not for others, as lack of motivation and possible failure do not help to develop confidence and self-esteem. Similarly, some people do not thrive in uncomfortable working environments or in jobs that they do not like, so your children should never be cajoled into doing something that really does not suit them. This could have a detrimental effect on their personal confidence and lower their self-esteem.

CASE STUDY

BT offers an apprenticeship programme that is very popular, with many more applicants than places available. However, it also offers placements for people who have decided that they would like to study for a degree, rather than take the apprenticeship route. Placements are offered for students who are in the penultimate year of their degree course and are available in three streams: professional services and customer experiences, ICT and functional specialist. Summer placements are available for 8 to 16 weeks between the months of June and September and industrial placements are available for 16 to 48 weeks. For more information about apprenticeships and graduate placements with BT, visit **www.btplc.com**.

Financial pros and cons

When thinking about the financial pros and cons, there are various research reports available that will help you to consider the issues and make decisions. For example, research conducted by the London School of Economics (LSE) found that by gaining a degree a woman can earn up to 26 per cent more than a woman who does not continue her education beyond A levels. A man can earn about 23 per cent more by completing a degree course. For more information about the LSE and their research, visit **www2.lse.ac.uk**.

However, if your children go to university they could graduate with a debt of at least £35,000. Their student loan will need to be paid back once they start earning £21,000 and this could be a long-term financial commitment. If, however, you have money to spare you could help your children by paying for tuition fees or maintenance, for example, which would reduce the amount of loan debt after they graduate. You and they need to discuss your attitude towards debt and decide whether the benefits of a university education outweigh this potential debt.

The National Apprenticeship Service (NAS) states that 'research shows that apprentices earn, on average, over £100,000 more throughout their lifetime than other employees'. It is not clear what research this is, or which other employees are compared with apprentices, or indeed what is meant by 'on average' so it is difficult to verify the accuracy of this statement. However, if your children obtain full-time employment or an apprenticeship they will be earning a wage from day one and, with careful financial management, they could begin to save money that could help them to obtain a mortgage in the future, for example. Also, they will not have to repay a student loan.

Career pros and cons

A survey by the Organization for Economic Co-operation and Development (OECD) found that graduates in OECD countries are more likely to find a job than non-graduates. For women, 78 per cent with a degree are in employment, compared with 63 per cent of women without a degree. For men, 89 per cent with a degree are in employment, compared with 84 per cent of men without a degree. For more information about the OECD and their research, visit **www.oecd.org**.

These statistics show that continuing into higher education enhances employment prospects significantly. It also widens career choices, opening up a larger selection of possible careers. However, the Association of Graduate Recruiters (AGR) has reported that, owing to the economic downturn, vacancies for graduates have fallen for the first time since 2003. Also, the government is considering cutting the number of university places along with the massive increase in tuition fees in 2012, so employment benefits should be weighed up against financial issues and practical issues of being able to secure a place. For more information about the AGR, visit **www.agr.org.uk**.

At this current time it is difficult to find reliable and verifiable statistics on the career benefits to be gained through undertaking a modern-day apprenticeship. Indeed, more research is needed to track the career progression of young people who have become apprentices. Despite the government and NAS providing a positive outlook on the scheme (and enthusiasm demonstrated by apprentices who took part in the research for this book), some people who work within the youth sector are a little more sceptical about the opportunities that are available for young people, as the following quotation illustrates.

CASE STUDY

I know the government is always very keen to get employers on board but there's always this, well how do I pay for an apprentice type thing. I know a lot of employers feel that they can't take a young person on or they'll say well you haven't got any experience. Well, where are they going to get the experience if you are not willing to take them on? So I don't know whether more apprenticeships will actually appear, definitely not in the near future, and possibly not in the long term if the government is trying to keep 14- to 19-year-olds in school or training of some form. But how they're going to make employers offer apprenticeships, I don't know.

SOURCE Petra, trainer and adviser, The Rendezvous, Sherborne

Encouraging effective decisions

One of the best ways to encourage your children to make effective decisions is to ask the right questions. If you do this well, your children will be able to think deeply about all the options and start to make some choices about their future career and the route they need to take to achieve their goals. There are many ways to ask questions that will stimulate thought. These include:

- Asking open questions that require more than one-word answers. Examples of open questions include those that begin with 'why', 'who', 'what' and 'how'.

- Asking questions that make your children think. When doing this, make sure that you give your children plenty of time to think and don't interrupt their thought process.

- Asking questions that stimulate reflection. Reflective thought involves the ability to acquire facts, understand ideas and arguments, analyse and evaluate information, weigh evidence, produce conclusions and make decisions. It includes the ability to question and solve problems by linking previous ideas, knowledge and experiences with present ideas, knowledge and experiences. This type of reflective thought is extremely useful to you and your children when thinking about career progression routes as you and they both then have plenty of experience and knowledge on which to draw.

- Asking relevant and 'real' questions that have meaning for your children. This could include, for example, helping your children to be realistic about their chances of obtaining a job/apprenticeship/ university place, based on their qualifications and previous work experience.

- Asking questions that test existing assumptions. This is of particular use in cases where your children are making assumptions about particular progression routes, without being able to back up their assumptions with evidence.

When asking your children questions to stimulate thought, there are certain types of question that should be avoided. These include:

- trick questions;
- biased questions;
- sterile questions that constrain thought;
- questions that are too simple, irrelevant or patronizing;
- questions for which the answer is readily available;
- emotive questions;
- closed questions that require only one-word answers.

CASE STUDY

NG Bailey, a UK-wide group of specialist mechanical, electrical, ICT, maintenance and building management companies, has been training apprentices since 1934. A purpose-built engineering academy was opened in 1969 and since then, over 4,000 men and women have successfully completed an apprenticeship programme, many of whom have won national and industry awards, and have progressed to take up senior management positions within the company.

Apprenticeships are offered in electrotechnical installation, heating and ventilation and building services engineering. Applications are usually open in January and February. However, competition for places can be fierce, with many more applicants than places available. For more information about apprentices with NG Bailey, visit **www.ngbailey.co.uk**.

Reaching consensus

It can be hard for parents and children to reach consensus, especially if you seem to have very different ideas about careers and progression routes. If you find that you are having difficulty, you can work through these difficulties in the following ways:

- Discuss the consequences of the decisions that your children are making at this stage of their lives. Again, try to do this in an unbiased way, encouraging your children to work out the consequences in their own way.

- Ask 'What if...?' This enables you to work through each option and reflect on how each choice could turn out in the future.

- Think about alternative ways to approach your difficulties in reaching consensus. Have a break, invite a third party to join discussions, or think about seeking professional advice (see Chapter 10).

- View the issue from various perspectives. Try to look at it from your children's perspective, and ask that they try to view it from your perspective.

- Break the problem down into manageable parts and omit irrelevant information. For example, if you are both agreed that certain progression routes are definitely not suitable, reduce the options to a manageable size.

- Try to supply alternatives or different outcomes.

- Try role play or role reversal.

- Recognize important questions to ask (see above).

CASE STUDY

Advanced Apprenticeships are available with Mercedes-Benz in the UK. They offer the following benefits:

- block training at the new Mercedes-Benz National Apprentice Academy in Milton Keynes;

- residential facilities with individual rooms and extensive pastoral care and supervision;

- a comprehensive practical training plan leading to nationally recognized qualifications;

- training on vehicles and diagnostic systems at the cutting edge of technology;

- full employment and a salary while training.

To find out more about these apprenticeships, or to hunt for a job with Mercedes-Benz, visit **www.mercedes-benz.motortrak.com/careers/apprentice.php**.

Avoiding arguments

If you follow all the advice offered in this chapter you should be able to have productive discussions with your children. In addition to this you can avoid arguments by taking notice of the following:

- Find the right time to hold a discussion. Don't do so when you and/or your children are tired or when any of you are busy or have an appointment, for example. Make sure that you have plenty of time available and that you won't be disturbed.

- Don't force your children into a discussion. Wait until they are happy to talk to you. If it appears that they do not want to discuss these issues with you, it may be possible to ask your spouse/partner or grandparents or siblings to broach the subject. Failing that, you may need to seek professional advice (see Chapter 10). As we can see from Michael's case study in Appendix 3, a local youth and advice centre provided all the help and support he needed during discussions about possible careers.

- Don't try to guilt-trip, cajole or bully your children into having a discussion or making decisions.

- Some young people know how they want their career to progress. If this is the case, and they are making sensible decisions, it may be prudent to let them make their own choices. Indeed, Laura demonstrates that she had unwavering support from her parents, whichever route she took, and that this support was extremely important to her (see Appendix 3). Steph also shows that she felt that she was mature enough to make her own sensible choices (see quotation below).

CASE STUDY

Thinking back, actually my mum and dad weren't that bothered, they left it up to me really. School helped a bit with my career choices but college was better. My tutor told me about university and I drove myself there when it was an Open Day. Mum and dad never came. Some of my mates had no end of trouble with their parents but I was alright. I went to Sheffield and it was great. Now I'm doing what I want. I didn't mind mum and dad not helping me. I was old enough to make my own choices really.

SOURCE Steph, IT manager, Sheffield

Summary

You can help your children to make decisions about their future career by providing unbiased, clear and accurate information in a non-confrontational way. You need to encourage your children to think about their future and to consider all the alternatives in relation to their wants, needs, skills, experiences and future hopes and aspirations. Arguments and confrontation can be avoided if you choose the right time to have the discussion and if you refrain from cajoling your children into doing something that they don't want to do. If you are unable to help them to reach a decision, you should seek professional advice.

If, after having discussed these issues, your children decide that they do wish to follow the apprenticeship route, it is useful to find out how you can support them as they embark on their apprenticeship programme. These issues are discussed in the following chapter.

Chapter Twelve
Supporting your children as apprentices

If your children decide that they would like to embark on an apprentice-ship programme, there are various ways that you can offer support. This includes helping with applications and interviews, helping with their accommodation needs, encouraging financial independence and responsibility, offering practical support and helping your children to remain motivated while they complete their apprenticeship programme. These issues are discussed in this chapter.

Helping with applications and interviews

Chapter 7 offers advice about applying for apprenticeships and includes information about filling in application forms, producing CVs, making the most of previous qualifications and experience, and attending interviews. You can help your children with their application and interview by encouraging them to read the information presented in Chapter 7. Also, you can use your skills and experience to help your children in practical ways, which could include the following:

- Edit and proof-read all written applications and CVs. Offer advice about content, layout, grammar and spelling.

- There are a variety of free CV templates available on the internet. Help your children to choose a suitable template that they can use to create their CV. Enter 'CV template' into your search engine to be directed to relevant pages.

- Direct your children to the BBC Student Life website (**www.bbc.co.uk/schools/studentlife**), which provides useful information about how to write a CV and attend an interview in the 'careers and choices' section.

- Once your children have sent out their CVs to local employers, encourage them to answer the telephone when it rings. Don't be tempted to speak to prospective employers on your children's behalf. During my research, employers said there is nothing worse than having a 'pushy' parent answer a telephone when they are ringing to speak to a candidate.

- Conduct mock interviews for your children, or ask a friend to undertake them for you.

- Offer advice about suitable attire for interviews. Some parents find it useful to go shopping (and pay) for their child's first interview outfit, if they can afford to do so. If your child is claiming Jobseeker's Allowance there is a grant available to cover the cost of formal interview attire. Also, if you are from a low-income household there may be grants available from local charities to help your children cover the costs associated with attending interviews. Contact your local authority, children's school or local parish for more information.

- Offer to help with transport to and from interviews if public transport is unavailable and/or your children do not have their own transport. Again, if you are from a low-income household, grants may be available in your area to cover the cost of transport to interviews.

Sorting out accommodation

As we saw in Chapter 1, it used to be the case that apprentices were offered accommodation for the duration of their apprenticeship. However, this is no longer the case. Today there are only a few programmes that provide accommodation for the whole apprenticeship and these tend to be in the leisure industry where apprentices are required to live and work onsite. If your children apply for such an apprenticeship, they should be encouraged to check the contract carefully to make sure that accommodation costs are covered and that there are no hidden extras. Some of these companies will also provide all meals: again, your children should check the contract to make sure that this is the case.

Living in the family home

If accommodation is not provided, and if the apprenticeship programme is available in your home town, you may decide that your children can live at home for the duration of the programme. Some parents decide to charge rent (full or minimal) to help their children understand the importance of paying for accommodation and to encourage good financial management (see below). Other parents are able and happy to provide free accommodation for the duration of the apprenticeship (see Laura's case study in Appendix 3).

Choosing private rented accommodation

Your children may need to find private rented accommodation. This could be because the apprenticeship programme is at a distance from your home town, they wish to become independent or you cannot afford to support them at home. When choosing private rented accommodation you should encourage your children to consider the following points:

- When viewing accommodation, they should check the locks. Do they look secure? Are there security bolts, window locks and door chains in place? Are there any tell-tale signs of recent break-ins, such as broken panes of glass, cracked door frames or broken locks? Are the boundaries to the property complete and secure? Would it be possible for somebody to climb over them easily? Is there public right of way near the property, such as alleyways or footpaths, which could pose a threat? Is the property overlooked by other properties that could provide extra security? Before choosing accommodation, encourage your children to consult **www.upmystreet.co.uk** to find out how the area performs on crime and policing.

- How much is the rent? Does the contract state start and finish dates, and clearly state how much rent is to be paid for this time? Check that the contract runs for the length of time that your children need for their apprenticeship programme (or that they will be able to renew the contract).

- Check the contract very carefully. If your children are to move in with other people, is the contract an individual or joint agreement? If it is an individual agreement your children are responsible only for their share of rent and bills. If it is a joint agreement they will be liable for everybody's rent and bills. Some landlords prefer to issue joint agreements because it covers them financially if someone in the house refuses to pay. However, it is not in your children's interests to be liable for everyone else's debt. Also, you should note that individual agreements will require all the tenants to purchase separate TV licences, whereas one licence will suffice for properties on which there is a joint agreement.

- How much is the deposit? Most private landlords will require a deposit, usually equivalent to one month's rent, and they will need to provide information about the tenancy deposit scheme that they intend to use (these schemes have been introduced to protect deposits and help to avoid disputes). They will also need to provide your children with a receipt for any money paid.

- Are bills included in the rent? If not, ask for a copy of previous bills so that you can work out how much your children will have to pay for utilities.

- What is to be provided in the property? The landlord should supply an up-to-date inventory that includes everything in the property and its condition. Ask to see the inventory and check that everything is available as described.

Accommodation while training

Although most apprenticeship programmes do not provide accommodation for the duration of the programme, many companies that have specialist training facilities for apprentices will provide accommodation while training takes place. This accommodation can be either purpose built and attached to the training site, or provided in local hotels. In these cases the employer pays all accommodation and costs, and may also pay for meals (see case studies, below). In other cases employers will meet all accommodation costs when an apprentice has to train away from their home town or has to travel on work business, but may not cover meals. Encourage your children to check all apprenticeship contracts to find out what expenses are covered.

CASE STUDY

Apprentices on the Suzuki Advanced Apprenticeship Programme undertake some of their training in block release at the Suzuki training facility. Hotel accommodation is provided for all apprentices so that they can live together and get to know each other. Members of the training staff carry out an induction to the hotel on first arrival and all Suzuki apprentices have a contact number for their trainer, who has responsibility for their pastoral care during block training.

Where Suzuki apprentices are travelling by train or coach, the Suzuki Advanced Apprenticeship Programme will arrange transport to the train/bus station and transport is provided from the hotel to the training centre.

Parents are informed immediately of any situations during residential training that are deemed to be the concern of a responsible parent. If trainees are caught in the possession of drugs they are sent home and parents and employers are informed immediately. For more information about the Suzuki Advanced Apprenticeship Programme, visit the 'learning' section of the Suzuki website: **www.suzuki-apprenticeships.co.uk**.

CASE STUDY

Seat provides hotel accommodation during off-the-job training. All hotels are selected using a standard checklist of minimum requirements. Each hotel has contact numbers for the vocational coaches and the programme manager. In addition to this, all trainees have a contact number for their vocational coach, who has responsibility for their pastoral care during training blocks.

All trainees are given clear guidance as to standards of acceptable behaviour while in residential accommodation. Trainees under the age of 18 will not be served alcohol in the hotel bar, and alcohol is not permitted in hotel rooms. Parents are notified of any problems that may be of importance to them and in the event of illness during residential training, the hotel, along with the programme staff, will ensure that appropriate medical treatment is sought. Trainees are asked to provide feedback on their hotel accommodation; this is evaluated and changes made where necessary. For more information about apprenticeships with Seat, visit **www.seat-apprenticeships.co.uk**.

Council tax

If your children are aged 18 or over they will be required to pay council tax. However, if they are doing an apprenticeship that leads to a recognized qualification, and provided they do not earn over a certain amount (currently £195 per week), they are not counted for council tax purposes. Therefore, if you are a single parent living on your own with your child, your household could receive a discount of 25 per cent on your council tax bill while your child is an apprentice. Also, if your child is living with one other adult (a partner or friend, for example) as the only adults in a property, the household could qualify for a 25 per cent discount on council tax. For more information about council tax, visit **www.direct.gov.uk/counciltax**.

Encouraging financial independence and responsibility

When your children first start to earn a wage, they may feel that they have much more money than they have ever had, even if they are only receiving the minimum apprenticeship wage of £2.60 an hour (see Chapter 3). If it is your intention that your children move out of the family home, or if they have to because the apprenticeship programme is at a distance from the family home, they will need to understand the importance of meeting their rent, utility and council tax commitments. Chapter 4 highlights the importance of making sure that your children are able to meet their basic needs, and Chapter 8 provides information about money management and working out a budget. Encourage them to read these chapters if you feel they need advice on these issues.

Lending money to your children

You may decide that you want to lend your children some money to help them to get established (or to pay a deposit on private rented accommodation, for example). If this is the case you need to make sure that they understand that you have made a loan rather than a gift. It is advisable to draw up a contract that is understood by your children, which clearly lays out the conditions of the loan and the repayment terms. Also, you should note that, if your children are still repaying your loan and want to take out a mortgage once they have finished their apprenticeship and obtained a well-paid job, the mortgage company may take the loan into account when assessing their application. They may request to see a copy of the contract and reduce the amount that they are willing to lend.

Giving money to your children

If you choose to make a financial gift to your children to help them to survive financially while on their apprenticeship programme, you will need to do so within the Inheritance Tax (IHT) rules. These rules state that where a gift has been made within seven years before the date of your death the gift must be added to your estate when calculating whether IHT is due, unless the gift is exempt from IHT (see below). Therefore, your children, as the recipients of your gift, may be liable to IHT on the gift if you should die within seven years of having given them the money. (IHT is paid on the estate of a person who has died if the taxable value of their estate is above £325,000: 2011/12 figures. The tax is paid only on the part of the estate that is above this limit: if your estate is worth less than this amount there is no IHT to pay. Currently, the rate of IHT is 40 per cent.)

However, there are exemptions available and if you make a financial gift to your children that is exempt, they will not have to pay IHT if you die within seven years. The three most relevant exemptions are:

- Small gifts of up to £250 can be made to as many people as you wish in any one tax year, which can include your children, although this small gift exemption cannot be used in conjunction with the annual exemption described below.

- An annual exemption of £3,000 per year can be given to your children. However, this cannot be used in conjunction with the small gift described above. This exemption can be carried forward for one year, meaning that you can give £6,000 in one tax year if you did not use your annual exemption in the previous year. As parents you should both remember to make use of your annual exemption. This could provide a significant amount of money to help your children financially, and can help you to reduce IHT liability on your death.

- Maintenance gifts of a 'reasonable amount' could be paid to your children if they are under the age of 18 or in full-time education. Although exact amounts aren't specified you could not give away more than what would be considered necessary for maintenance purposes to your children. This rule could be applied if your children are enrolled on a Young Apprenticeship or Programme-Led Apprenticeship, for example (see Chapter 2).

When making any of the above gifts you will need to keep careful records that can be given to the tax office to prove that the gifts have been made in a manner that is exempt from IHT. Rules can be complex, so if in doubt you should seek advice from a professional who is experienced in IHT rules and regulations. You can find an experienced adviser in your area by using the search facility available on the Chartered Institute of Taxation website: **www.tax.org.uk** (use the drop-down menu to search by 'inheritance tax').

Offering practical support

In addition to the financial support described above, there are practical ways that you can help your children when they enrol on an apprenticeship programme. This includes the following:

- Providing items for accommodation such as old crockery, cutlery, bed linen and cleaning utensils, if relevant.

- Offering cooking and healthy eating advice (some parents are happy to continue cooking for their children while on the apprenticeship programme, whereas others feel that they should learn to fend for themselves).

- Providing a laundry service (some parents are happy to wash and iron their children's clothes, whereas others feel that once their children enter the world of work they should do their own laundry). If your children are to live in private rented accommodation, make sure that there is a washing machine provided, which should be the case in furnished or semi-furnished accommodation.

- Offering advice, encouragement and support. Undertaking an apprenticeship can be a new and daunting experience for some young people, and having support and encouragement from parents can make a big difference (see quotation below and Laura's case study in Appendix 3).

- Helping with travel when required (see quotation below and Michael's case study in Appendix 3).

CASE STUDY

I shouldn't laugh, but she's not the most motivated. My husband and I would have to take her in in the mornings because she'd miss the bus left to herself. It's only four miles so not too bad. So there was that and I also had to talk to her when she thought she made a big mistake... she was talking about packing it all in. But I told her we all make mistakes but we learn from them. I told her she won't do that again, so she should put it all down to learning something new... yes, it did help her and she went back much happier.

SOURCE Sarah, mother of an 18-year-old apprentice in Northamptonshire

Helping your children to remain motivated

You can help your children to remain motivated by taking note of the following advice:

- Your children will find it easier to remain motivated if they enjoy their work and are interested in what they are learning. Therefore, you should help them to make careful choices about their apprenticeship. They shouldn't choose a programme purely because they think it will make you happy, for example.

- Your children need to enjoy the way that their training is delivered. They should try to choose an apprenticeship that offers the type of training that suits the way they like to learn, for example in block or on day release, at a college with other apprentices, or on their own with their mentor. If they are unhappy with the training they are receiving, they should speak to their training adviser (see Chapter 8).

- Encourage your children to set goals and make challenges for themselves. Try to encourage them to become active in the learning process.

- Encourage your children to recognize the transferable skills that they are gaining from their training and work experience (see Chapter 8).

- Help them to realize the importance of maintaining their health: encourage them to maintain a good diet, get plenty of sleep, get plenty of exercise and avoid marathon study or work sessions.

- If your children are living at home, provide them with a work space that is free from distractions and disturbance and make sure that siblings don't interfere with their work and IT equipment (see below).

CASE STUDY

I work in HR so I know all about work space and the importance of it. My daughter has got a lot of studying to do so I've given her my office while she's doing the apprenticeship. As I said before, she's not the most motivated person so I thought it would help her. Her sister isn't allowed to go near her laptop and I've even stopped the cat going in there because Sophie gets asthma. So the room is for her and nobody's allowed to go near her when she's in there.

SOURCE Sarah, mother of an 18-year-old apprentice in Northamptonshire

Summary

As a parent you may want to offer as much support as possible to your children when they embark on an apprenticeship programme. This can include utilizing your skills and experiences to provide advice and guidance when completing application forms and CVs and when attending interviews. You may also want to help your children by providing reduced-cost or free accommodation, lending money or providing cash gifts to help them meet costs such as accommodation, utilities and food. As a parent you also understand the importance of offering emotional support when required.

This section of the book has provided advice and guidance to parents who have children who are thinking about embarking on an apprenticeship programme. The next section will go on to offer advice for jobseekers and career changers who are thinking about undertaking an apprenticeship.

Part Four
Information for jobseekers and career changers

Chapter Thirteen
Is an apprenticeship the right route?

The following section of the book is aimed at jobseekers and career changers. If you fall into either of these categories and you are thinking about embarking on an apprenticeship programme, you need to make sure that it is the right route for you to take. When doing this you may find it beneficial to obtain advice and guidance from a professional advice worker, in addition to finding out all you can about apprenticeships. You will also need to consider the personal benefits, the financial implications, age-related issues and ask the right questions to aid decision making. These issues are discussed in this chapter.

Obtaining advice and guidance

As an adult who is thinking about changing careers or who is not in employment at this present time, there are two main types of professional advice that you can seek. The first is general advice about all the options that are available, including different types of employment, education and training. The second is information specifically about apprenticeships.

General advice

If you are in any doubt about whether an apprenticeship is the right route for you to take, you may find it useful to seek professional advice from an advice worker who is able to offer advice about all the career and education options that are available. The following organizations provide this kind of general advice:

- If you live in Scotland, contact your local Careers Scotland Centre for advice and guidance about career options. You can find your nearest centre by using the postcode search available on the Careers Scotland website: **www.careers-scotland.org.uk**. The website also contains useful information about planning a career, what to do if you are facing redundancy, researching a career and education options. Alternatively, you can obtain information and advice by telephoning 0845 8 502 502.

- If you live in Wales, contact your local Careers Wales centre. There are six Careers Wales companies covering the Welsh regions. Contact details and telephone numbers of each company can be obtained from the Careers Wales website: **www.careerswales.com**. Alternatively, you can telephone the national helpline: Learning and Careers Advice 0800 100 900. You can also e-mail lca@careerswales.com for more information.

- If you live in Northern Ireland, contact your local careers office for more information and advice. Contact details can be obtained from the Careers Service Northern Ireland website: **www.careersserviceni.com**. There is plenty of useful information on this website, including information about choosing a career, writing a CV, attending interviews, taking part in training courses and applying for college and university.

- If you live in England, contact your local Next Step service, which provides careers advice for adults (aged 19 or over. If you are below this age see Chapter 4). You can obtain contact details of your local Next Step service by using the map available on the Next Step website: **https://nextstep.direct.gov.uk**. The website also contains information about planning a career, undertaking an apprenticeship and funding further study. It is possible to e-mail an adviser or telephone 0800 100 900 for specific advice and guidance or to arrange a face-to-face meeting.

- Jobcentre Plus is a government agency that is part of the Department for Work and Pensions (DWP). Its role is to support people of working age from welfare into work and to help to fill vacancies advertised by employers. You can use the postcode search facility on the website to find contact details of your nearest Jobcentre Plus office: **www.jobcentreplus.gov.uk**. If you are not in paid employment you can obtain more advice from your personal adviser to find out about the various career, education and training options that are available.

Apprenticeship advice

Information specifically about apprenticeships can be obtained from the following websites:

- **www.apprenticeships.org.uk**. This is the website of the National Apprenticeship Service (NAS). On this site you can find out more about all types of apprenticeship in England and use the database to access information about apprenticeship vacancies. Information is available for apprentices, parents, employers, college staff and advisers.

- **www.skillsdevelopmentscotland.co.uk**. This is the website of Skills Development Scotland (SDS), which is Scotland's skills public body that operates across Scotland as a whole. On this site you can find out more about Modern Apprenticeships and access some interesting case studies.

- **www.delni.gov.uk/apprenticeshipsni**. This is the apprenticeship section of the website of the Department for Employment and Learning in Northern Ireland. Visit this site for more information about apprenticeships in Northern Ireland, including information about the different types that are available and interesting case studies.

- **http://wales.gov.uk**. This is the website of the Welsh Assembly Government. Enter 'apprenticeships' into the search box to find information about the various apprenticeship schemes that are available in Wales.

- **www.sscalliance.org**. This is the website of the Alliance of Sector Skills Councils. SSCs provide information about apprenticeships in their sector, so visit the above website for links to the relevant SSC website, or see Appendix 4 for contact details of each SSC. More information about SSCs can be obtained from Chapter 1.

- **www.horsesmouth.co.uk**. This website provides a social network for informal mentoring and has been formed in partnership with the NAS 'to encourage people who have been through an apprenticeship to mentor and inspire others in a safe and friendly social online environment'. Visit this site for up-to-date advice about apprenticeships and to find a mentor.

If you require specific advice about the type of apprenticeships that are available in your area, you can arrange to speak to an adviser at your local college or training centre. You should note, however, that this person will only be able to offer advice about apprenticeship programmes provided by their organization and will not be able to offer general advice about the other options that are available. You can also contact your regional Apprenticeship Training Agency (ATA) for more information about apprenticeships in your area (see Chapter 1 for contact details).

CASE STUDY

Škoda provides an Advanced Apprenticeship programme that is designed to train and develop apprentices in a way that enables them to keep pace with advancing technology and high levels of customer service. The programme is for three years and leads to an NVQ Level 3, an IMI Technical Certificate, an Advanced Apprenticeship Completion Certificate and Key and Core Skills Certificates relevant to the specialist area. On completion of the apprenticeship candidates can progress through the Škoda Qualification Programme on the route to becoming a master technician.

Candidates must be aged 16 or over and have GCSEs in maths, English and an IT subject at, ideally, Grade C or above, or a Scottish Certificate of Education Standard Grade 3 or above. Škoda apprentice technicians follow a programme of theory and practical training. This involves interactive classroom study and hands-on experience in the workshops, as well as online. All qualification fees, training courses and accommodation are paid by Škoda. For more information about the Advanced Apprenticeship programme with Škoda, visit **www.skoda-apprenticeships.co.uk**.

Understanding the personal benefits

Apprenticeships enable you to improve your skills and gain qualifications that are nationally recognized. More qualifications and improved skills enable you to choose from a wider variety of jobs and may help you to gain promotion and a higher salary. If you are a jobseeker these qualifications and the work experience that you gain from your apprenticeship programme should help you to obtain full-time employment in the future. Also, apprenticeships can enable you to develop your skills and personal confidence and can be of great value to people who been out of work for a while and who may be lacking in confidence within the workplace and within a training environment.

However, it is important that you think about your training needs in terms of other options that are available to you. For example, if you are thinking about changing careers, have you considered education courses that could be more appropriate to your needs? A part-time foundation degree (undertaken while you are working) could enable you to change careers or help you to progress to a full Bachelor's degree (see Chapter 14). As a career changer, you need to make sure that your training needs are met in the best and most efficient way. For more information about foundation degrees, visit **http://fd.ucas.com**.

When considering whether an apprenticeship is the right route to take, you also need to think about how the programme will help you to develop, personally. If you have not taken part in any training courses since having left school, an apprenticeship may provide the opportunity for you to embark on a training programme in a supportive environment with other people with similar wants and needs. It is of particular use to people who want to train while they are working, and provides the opportunity for training to be directly related to your work. However, if you want to spend more time studying, and less time in full-time employment, perhaps there might be a better route such as part-time employment combined with part-time study at college or university (see Chapter 14). More information about the advantages and disadvantages of embarking on an apprenticeship programme is provided in Chapters 4 and 10.

Choosing the right level of apprenticeship

Whether a jobseeker or a career changer, you also need to ensure that you choose an apprenticeship that is at the right level as this will help you to develop your skills and will be of most benefit to your personal career. In most cases this will be dictated by the entry qualifications and experience required for the position. However, if you are in any doubt about which level is suitable, you should seek professional advice from the relevant organization listed above. More information about the different levels of apprenticeship is provided in Chapter 2.

CASE STUDY

The RAF offers a wide variety of apprenticeships for people who want to complete a UK-recognized trade apprenticeship while they are training or working in the RAF. Apprenticeships are offered in the following areas:

- engineering and technical;
- catering and hospitality;

- security and defence;
- personnel support;
- air operations support;
- communications and intelligence;
- logistics and equipment.

Apprenticeships can last from six months to three years and pay, after one year, will be at least £17,140 (2011/12 figures). Other benefits include subsidized food and accommodation, free medical and dental care and access to free gym and sports facilities. For more information about apprenticeships with the RAF, visit **www.raf.mod.uk/careers/jobs/apprenticeships**.

Understanding the financial implications

An apprenticeship offers you the chance to train while you are working and receive a wage from the first day of employment. As we have seen in Chapter 3, from October 2011 all apprentices aged under 19 and apprentices aged 19 or over who are in the first year of their apprenticeship are paid an hourly rate of £2.60, although employers can pay above this amount, if they wish. All apprentices over the age of 19 who have completed the first year of their apprenticeship are entitled to the National Minimum Wage (NMW) appropriate for their age (£6.08 for workers aged 21 and over and £4.98 for workers aged 18–20).

If you are currently out of work and claiming benefits, you need to consider how your income from benefits will be affected by becoming an apprentice. Also, there are other sources of help that you may be entitled to, such as a Job Grant that is tax-free and does not affect other benefits or tax credits, and the In Work Credit, which is a fixed tax-free payment of £40 per week (£60 per week in London) for parents bringing up children alone. You will need to check whether it is possible to qualify for this type of financial aid on the particular apprenticeship programme that you choose (your personal adviser will be able to offer advice about this). If you qualify for the Job Grant you will be eligible for Extended Council Tax Benefit and Extended Housing Benefit. More information about these benefits can be obtained from the government information website (**www.direct.gov.uk**), from your local benefits office or from your local Jobcentre Plus office.

If you are already in employment and are thinking about changing careers or asking your current employer if you can embark on an apprenticeship programme, in some cases you may have to take a drop in salary. Again, you need to work out whether this move is financially feasible and weigh up the benefits of embarking on the programme with any financial loss that you may incur.

CASE STUDY

Tesco offers an apprenticeship in retail that lasts for a year. It leads to an NVQ in Retail Level 2, Key Skills Levels 1 or 2 (depending on whether candidates already have GCSEs in English and maths), and a Technical Certificate in Retail Level 2. To qualify for the scheme, candidates must be a Tesco employee, work more than 18 hours a week and have been a UK resident for three years with indefinite leave to remain, or have asylum seeker status. The scheme is not open to people who are in full-time education or who are planning to return to full-time education. For more information about this apprenticeship scheme, visit **www.tesco-careers.com**.

Understanding age-related issues

As we have seen in Chapter 3, colleges and training providers often advertise their apprenticeships only for people of certain age groups, because younger people attract more government funding for their training (and government funding for apprenticeships is exempt from age discrimination legislation). Unfortunately, there is nothing that can be done about this and if you fall outside the advertised age group you will not be able to apply for a funded place on these apprenticeship programmes.

However, since the introduction of age discrimination legislation in 2006, employers are no longer able to specify specific age groups when recruiting unless they can demonstrate legitimate reasons to discriminate on the grounds of age (see below). Employers must also take care to ensure that the recruitment process for attracting and recruiting apprentices does not discriminate against older workers. They must not use words in job advertisements that are discriminatory, such as 'this position is suitable for a school leaver' or 'only applicants over the age of 21 need apply'.

Objective justification for discrimination

According to the Equality and Human Rights Commission, employers must be able to demonstrate that discrimination is 'proportionate' and contributes to a 'legitimate' aim. Proportionate means that:

- The action of the employer must achieve its aim.

- The discriminatory effect should be outweighed significantly by the importance and benefits of the legitimate aim.

- The employer should have no reasonable alternative to the action they are taking. If the legitimate aim can be achieved by different (and less discriminatory) means, they must then opt for that route.

Legitimate means:

- economic factors such as the needs of and the efficiency of running a business;

- the health, welfare and safety of the individual (including protection of young people or older workers);

- the particular training requirements of the job.

If you feel that an employer does not have objective justification for discrimination, it is possible to take legal action and the onus is on the employer to demonstrate that restricting the age range of applicants was justified. For example, local authorities could argue that they are taking on younger apprentices because they are trying to address the high levels of youth unemployment in their area. It would be up to the courts to weigh up the evidence and decide whether or not this is a legitimate aim and whether the local authority could adopt a different strategy to achieve this aim. More information about these rules can be obtained from the Equality and Human Rights Commission website: **www.equalityhumanrights.com**.

Avoiding age discrimination rules

Employers have found a way to overcome age discrimination rules. In some cases they advertise an apprenticeship to all age groups, but when an older candidate steps forward they point out that there is no government funding available for the apprenticeship and that the candidate will need to pay for their own training, or, in some cases, work for free (see Laura's case study, in Appendix 3). This can put off a lot of applicants because they cannot afford to pay for their training or work without receiving a wage.

However, since the employer has offered the position to all age groups it is not seen as age discrimination by either the government or the employer. Although this situation is very unsatisfactory for people over the age of 18, some apprenticeship providers hope that these problems will be overcome with extra funding for Adult Apprenticeships. (Vince Cable, the Business Secretary, announced his intention to expand the number of Adult Apprenticeships available by 75,000 in 2014–15, meaning that there will be a total of 200,000 adults starting their apprenticeship in that year. The government will be investing £605 million in Adult Apprenticeships in 2011–12.)

Despite these funding issues and complex age discrimination rules, many older people do succeed in obtaining an apprenticeship, as the example from The Age and Employment Network (TAEN) illustrates below.

CASE STUDY

TAEN reports that provisional figures for the period from August to October 2010 reveal that just over 8,500 (7.1 per cent) of almost 120,000 people starting apprenticeships during those three months were aged 45 and over. This compares with a total of 10,210 people aged 45+ (3.65 per cent of the total) who started apprenticeships during the full 2009/10 academic year.

Also, according to figures obtained by Age UK and TAEN from the Skills Funding Agency, the number of 50+ apprentices leapt from 2,605 in 2007/08 to 5,376 in 2008/09. This figure includes over 400 people in their sixties and 13 in their seventies, including the oldest apprentice in the country aged 76. For more information about TAEN and their research, visit **http://taen.org.uk**. For more information about Age UK, visit **www.ageuk.org.uk**.

Using an apprenticeship to change career

People decide to change careers for a variety of reasons. Perhaps you are bored with your current job and see no future, or perhaps you believe that you have skills and talents that are not being utilized. Apprenticeship programmes can provide the opportunity for you to change your career, sometimes in quite a dramatic way. If you are thinking about doing this, the following points may help:

- Make sure that you have undertaken thorough research about your future career direction. Seek professional advice where appropriate (see above). Don't make decisions based on inaccurate information or preconceptions about a different career path. All decisions you make must be backed up by appropriate evidence and accurate information.

- Don't rush your decisions. This can be tempting if you really dislike your current job. However, decisions made in haste can turn out to be disastrous, and you could find yourself on an apprenticeship programme that is not what you expected and is no better than your current role. Again, seek professional advice as guidance workers will be able to present all the options and discuss each of these in terms of your personal career path.

- You need to make sure that you are not taking a step backwards in your career, unless the apprenticeship is something that you really want to do and will provide the opportunity to start again on a totally different career path. If this is the case, undertake careful research to ensure that you choose the right programme and make sure that you fully understand what your new career path will entail.

- Make sure that you are accepted onto an appropriate apprenticeship programme before you hand in your notice for your current job and that there is no chance that the offer will be withdrawn. Some employers will not hold your job open for you, should the apprenticeship offer fall through.

CASE STUDY

Siemens offers a wide variety of apprenticeships in areas such as energy service (gas and wind turbine manufacturing), transportation systems, traffic controls, IT solutions and services, commercial academy and transmission and distribution (power station and electricity supply). The length of apprenticeship and amount of salary vary depending on the sector. Minimum requirements for entry are GCSEs (or equivalent) in maths, English and science, although some sectors will also require A levels. ICT qualifications will be advantageous.

Although application procedures vary, depending on the sector, in general you will need to apply online, undertake psychometric testing, attend an assessment centre and complete an interview. To find out more about these apprenticeships and for information about how to apply online, visit **www.siemens.co.uk**.

Asking the right questions

When deciding whether an apprenticeship is the right progression route you should consider the following questions. Try to answer 'yes' to as many questions as possible, as this will help to ensure that you make the right decisions. If you answer 'no' to any questions, you may need to undertake more research before making your decisions (see Chapter 14 for more information about all the options that are available).

		Yes	No
1	Have you sought advice from an experienced professional?	☐	☐
2	Have you found out all you can about the options that are available?	☐	☐
3	Do you understand what the different options entail?	☐	☐
4	Do you understand how each option could help your career to progress?	☐	☐
5	Do you understand how each option could help your personal development?	☐	☐
6	Do you know about the types of qualification that are available in each option?	☐	☐
7	Will these qualifications help you to progress in your career?	☐	☐
8	Do you have the right level of qualifications/experience to apply?	☐	☐
9	Do you need to gain any further qualifications or experience?	☐	☐
10	Have you considered the financial implications of each option?	☐	☐
11	If changing careers, can you afford to do so?	☐	☐
12	If you are a jobseeker, have you considered the effect on your benefits?	☐	☐
13	Have you looked into whether you qualify for any additional financial help?	☐	☐

		Yes	No
14	Do you know how to apply for this additional financial help?	☐	☐
15	Have you discussed all the options with partners, family and/or friends?	☐	☐
16	Do you have the required support from partners, family and/or friends?	☐	☐

Summary

When thinking about whether an apprenticeship is the right progression route it is important to find out as much information as possible from reliable sources. Much of this information is available online. It is also useful to obtain advice and guidance tailored specifically to your needs, and this can be done by accessing your local careers service. When thinking about the options, you need to make sure that you have the right qualifications and experience to apply, that you can afford to embark on your chosen programme and that you understand what personal benefits will be gained.

In order to be able to consider whether an apprenticeship programme is a good option, you need to know about alternative routes, which can include various training schemes, different education programmes and other types of employment. These issues are discussed in the following chapter.

Chapter Fourteen
Knowing about the alternatives

In order to make an informed choice about whether an apprenticeship is the right route for you to take, you need to know more about the alternative routes that are available. This involves gaining a clear understanding of British qualifications, understanding more about the types of organization that provide training and education courses, considering the different options that are available if you decide to remain with your current employer and knowing about employment training schemes if you are currently out of work. These issues are discussed in this chapter.

Understanding British qualifications

If you are interested in improving your qualifications it is useful to know what types of qualification are available, especially as some of these may have changed since you were in full-time education. Qualifications that you may be interested in are listed below.

A levels (AS and A2)

The Advanced Level General Certificate of Education (A level) is a qualification offered by education institutions in England, Northern Ireland and Wales and by a small minority of institutions in Scotland. The qualification is a two-tier system in which students study for the AS level in the first year. The AS level is a qualification in its own right so students can decide to finish their studies after having completed the first year. If students want to obtain the full A level, they go on to study the A2 level in the second year.

The A2 level, however, is not a qualification in its own right. A and AS levels are graded A* – E and grades can earn UCAS Tariff points that are added together and used for entry into higher education. For more information about UCAS Tariff, visit **www.ucas.com/students/ucas_tariff**.

Applied AS/A levels

These qualifications are designed to offer more emphasis on vocational education and training, encouraging students to foster links with employers and work as part of a team. They include subjects such as applied art and design, applied business and applied ICT. Some universities will accept applied A levels for entry, whereas others will not (it tends to be the more vocational university courses that will accept applied A levels). Visit the UCAS website (details above) to find out whether a course in which you are interested will accept applied A levels as an entry qualification.

14–19 Diplomas

These qualifications were launched in 2008 in England to provide an alternative qualification for school and college students. A variety of subjects are being introduced over a four-year period until 2012, but all diplomas will include core skills such as English, maths and ICT. Diplomas have been awarded points for the UCAS Tariff system, which means that an advanced diploma can be used for entry to university. However, you should check that this is the case because some university courses will not recognize the qualification for entry. There are three levels available:

- foundation (equivalent to Level 1 or 5 GCSEs at Grade D – G);
- higher (equivalent to Level 2 or 7 GCSEs at Grade A* – C);
- advanced (equivalent to Level 3 or 3.5 A levels).

International Baccalaureate

This qualification was taken by children who lived overseas with their families. However, some colleges are now adopting the qualification in the UK. It is recognized internationally and is broadly equivalent to three A levels. Most universities accept the International Baccalaureate (IB) as an entry qualification. More information about the IB can be obtained from **www.ibo.org**.

Scottish National Qualifications

These qualifications are available for students studying in Scotland. They provide a broad range of options for progression from Standard Grade and are available at five different levels – Access, Intermediate 1, Intermediate 2, Higher and Advanced Higher. The qualifications are made up of three units and each of these units is a qualification in its own right. Students are able to build up National Qualifications and Units into Scottish Group Awards. These are larger qualifications built up unit by unit and can be equivalent to degrees, diplomas, HNDs etc. More information about Scottish qualifications can be obtained from **www.sqa.org.uk**.

National Vocational Qualifications

These qualifications are work-related, competence-based vocational qualifications. A list of competencies in a particular occupation is drawn up and a person has to demonstrate that they can meet the competence level required. Most NVQs are studied by people in full-time employment, although some can be studied at college with off-site training. Also, they can be studied as part of an apprenticeship programme. There are five different levels of NVQ:

- NVQ Level 1 = GCSE D/E grades;
- NVQ Level 2 = GCSE C grade;
- NVQ Level 3 = A level;
- NVQ Level 4 = Bachelor's degree/HND;
- NVQ Level 5 = postgraduate diploma/degree or professional qualification.

More information about NVQs is provided in Chapter 5.

City & Guilds qualifications

City & Guilds provide vocational awards in over 400 work-related areas. They are designed to recognize skills used in the workplace and prove a person has practical skills in addition to theoretical knowledge. City & Guilds qualifications are available at a number of different levels in many occupations, ranging from catering to plumbing. They can be studied as part of an apprenticeship programme. More information about City & Guilds qualifications can be obtained from **www.cityandguilds.com**.

Access to higher education

Access courses are provided for people who wish to enter higher education through a route other than A levels. They tend to be designed for older students who wish to return to education after a break. Access courses can be studied full-time over one year, or part-time over two years. Successful completion of an access course leads to a 'kite-marked' award. The awards qualify students for entry into higher education. To find out more about access courses visit **www.accesstohe.ac.uk**.

BTEC (Edexcel)

This is a nationally recognized examining body which specializes in courses linked to commerce and industry. BTEC courses are suitable, in particular, if you have a good idea of your future career. BTEC National Diplomas, Advanced Diplomas and National Certificates are available in a variety of subjects ranging from construction to sports and exercise science. It is possible to take BTEC qualifications as part of an apprenticeship pro-gramme. More information about BTEC (Edexcel) can be obtained from **www.edexcel.com**.

National Open College Network

The National Open College Network (NOCN) was established in 1986. It is a provider of accreditation services for adult learning and is a major National Qualification awarding body, offering qualifications from Entry Level to Level Three/Advanced in a wide range of subjects. NOCN qualifi-cations are suitable for people who do not wish to follow traditional academic routes. Students are able to build up credits, accumulating and transferring the credits according to their needs. They are available at the following levels:

- Entry level: this measures individual progress, particularly in basic skills and self-confidence.
- Level 1: broadly comparable to NVQ Level 1 and GCSE Grades D to G.
- Level 2: broadly comparable to NVQ Level 2 and GCSE Grades A to C.
- Level 3: broadly comparable to NVQ Level 3 and A Levels.

For more information about NOCN qualifications, visit **www.nocn.org.uk**.

Higher National Diploma and Higher National Certificate

These qualifications are advanced, vocational courses that relate to a particular occupation or field. The Higher National Certificate (HNC) usually takes one year to complete on a full-time basis and two years on a part-time basis. The Higher National Diploma (HND) is at a higher level and usually takes two years to complete on a full-time basis and three to four years on a part-time basis. Some people choose to continue on to a degree course after completing an HND, and may be able to join the degree course in the second year. It may be possible to study for these qualifications as part of a higher-level apprenticeship.

Diploma/Certificate of Higher Education

These qualifications are offered by many HE institutions and tend to be academic, rather than vocational (they can be viewed as academic versions of the HNC and HND described above). The certificate is generally studied over one year full-time and the diploma usually takes two years of full-time study, although both can be studied part-time. Following the completion of a Diploma or Certificate in Higher Education, students gain credits that can be built up towards a Bachelor's degree course at a later stage.

Foundation degree

Foundation degrees combine academic studies with workplace learning. They take two years to complete and provide a qualification in their own right (recognized by employers) or can be used as a stepping stone to a full degree. It may be possible to study for a foundation degree as part of a higher-level apprenticeship. More information about foundation degrees can be obtained from **http://fd.ucas.com**.

Bachelor's degree

Most HE courses lead to a Bachelor's degree (also called an undergraduate degree, ordinary degree or first degree). This could be a Bachelor of Arts (BA), a Bachelor of Science (BSc) or a Bachelor of Education (BEd), for example. Most Bachelor's degree courses tend to be taught over three years for full-time study, although some full-time degree courses can last for four years, with one year for work or study placement. Alternatively, degrees can be taken part-time and can take up to five years to complete.

In many HE institutions subjects are now studied in modules. This means that you can study a variety of modules that make up your degree. In a standard year you would need to complete 120 credits by studying a selection of modules, each worth anything from 10 credits upwards. Some institutions, however, tend to follow a more traditional, single subject course of study, or specify the amount and type of modules that can be taken together.

Postgraduate certificates and diplomas

These qualifications are available for people who wish to study at a level higher than Bachelor's degree (see above). They can be academic or vocational and are studied over one year full-time, over two years on a part-time basis or through distance learning over a longer period of time. The certificate is at a lower level than the diploma. These qualifications are available in a wide range of subjects and can be a course in their own right or can be part of a Master's course (see below). Usually you will need to have a Bachelor's degree to study on one of these courses, although this is not always the case, especially if you have the relevant work experience at the right level.

Professional Graduate and Postgraduate Certificate in Education

These qualifications are available in England and Wales and are for people who wish to go into teaching. The Professional Graduate Certificate in Education is the same level academically as the final year of a Bachelor's degree course, whereas the Postgraduate Certificate in Education contains credits at final year Bachelor's degree level and some at Master's degree level (the postgraduate course is more academically challenging). The courses are generally either one year full-time or two years for part-time study and students are required to carry out a good deal of classroom practice during their course. In Scotland you can study for a Professional Graduate Diploma of Education (PGDE).

Master's degree

These degrees tend to be studied by people who have already received a Bachelor's degree, although adults who are able to demonstrate a suitable level of work experience and competence may be admitted to a course without a first degree. Master's degrees are either taught full-time for one year or part-time for two/three years, although some institutions will offer the courses through distance learning for a longer period of time. Some Master's courses are not taught courses but are research courses, which means that a student undertakes a piece of independent research, usually over two years.

Master of Business Administration (MBA)

This is a qualification for people who are interested in management and business. Applicants who are able to demonstrate the required level of experience and competence will be accepted on to a course without a Bachelor's degree. Courses can be studied full-time over one year, part-time over two years or through distance learning over a longer period of time. Part-time courses are becoming increasingly popular as people can combine the course with employment. Evening classes or distance learning also make studying for an MBA easier for employed adults.

Doctor of Philosophy

Studying for a postgraduate doctorate involves in-depth research into a specific topic, decided upon by the student or institution (this qualification can be abbreviated as PhD, Ph.D, D.Phil or Dr). Entrants will need a Bachelor's degree or a Master's degree to be accepted on to a doctorate programme. A student might conduct the research over a three- or four-year period full-time or part-time over four to five years, although some people take much longer to obtain their doctorate. There are also 'new route' PhDs available, which enable students to combine a specific research project with a coherent programme of formal course work and professional skills development.

Qualification frameworks

In England, Northern Ireland and Wales there are three frameworks that enable you to find out how different qualifications compare with each other, and help you to understand how you can progress from one qualification to another:

- The National Qualifications Framework (NQF) sets out the level at which a qualification can be recognized and helps you to make informed decisions about the qualifications you need. By using this framework you can compare the levels of different qualifications and identify clear progression routes for your chosen career. For more information about the NQF and to view the framework, visit **www.ofqual.gov.uk**. This is the website of the Office of Qualifications and Examinations Regulation, which is responsible for regulation of general and vocational qualifications in England and vocational qualifications in Northern Ireland.

● The Qualifications and Credit Framework (QCF) contains new vocational (or work-related) qualifications, available in England, Wales and Northern Ireland. It is a flexible framework that allows you to gain qualifications at your own pace along routes that suit your personal needs. For more information about this framework, visit the education and learning section on the government information website: **www.direct.gov.uk**.

● The Framework for Higher Education Qualifications (FHEQ) has been designed by the HE sector, and describes all the main HE qualifications. It applies to degrees, diplomas, certificates and other academic awards granted by a university or HE college (apart from honorary degrees and higher doctorates). For more information, visit **www.qaa.ac.uk**.

If you live in Scotland the Scottish Credit and Qualifications Framework (SCQF) provides a framework for qualifications in Scotland. Visit **www.scqf.org.uk** for more information.

Knowing about learning providers

If you are interested in taking any of the qualifications described above and/or developing your skills and knowledge, there are various types of learning provider offering such courses, as described below:

● FE colleges offer a wide range of courses to students of all ages. Courses can be during the day, during the evening, full-time, part-time, day release or block release. Qualifications can be academic or vocational. You can obtain details of your local FE college by visiting the Association of Colleges website: **www.aoc.co.uk**.

● Specialist colleges offer further education in specific areas such as art and design, music, agriculture or childcare. Courses can be full-time or part-time and some courses are residential with a bursary included. More information about these colleges and bursaries can be obtained from **http://moneytolearn.direct.gov.uk/residentialbursary**.

- Private training organizations offer courses at FE level and many offer vocational training courses (including apprenticeships) that may be open to people who are currently out of work (see below). Some of these organizations have charitable status and some attract government funding for their courses. Contact details can be obtained from your local telephone directory.

- Adult residential colleges offer short and long courses for adults in a supportive, residential environment in subjects such as art, computing, languages, history, social studies and music. Accommodation and meals are provided, and bursaries may be available for students from low-income households. More information about these colleges can be obtained from **www.arca.uk.net**.

- The Workers' Educational Association (WEA) is a registered charity that offers courses throughout the UK. More information about the WEA can be obtained from **www.wea.org.uk**. You can use the course search facility available at **https://enrolonline.wea.org.uk** to find out what courses are provided close to your home.

- An adult education service may be available in your area, run by your local authority. This service provides courses aimed specifically at adults. Some may lead to vocational qualifications, others to academic qualifications, or many courses are offered for interest, without leading to a specific qualification. Contact your local authority direct for information about their adult education service.

- Colleges of higher education offer foundation degrees, Bachelor's degrees and access courses on a full-time and part-time basis. Some of these are called colleges of further and higher education and will also offer courses at further education level, similar to the general FE colleges described above. For more information about colleges of higher education, visit **www.ucas.ac.uk**.

- Universities, including traditional universities, new universities and former polytechnics, all offer undergraduate and postgraduate courses on a full-time and part-time basis. Many universities also have an adult education department (sometimes called the adult continuing education department or the extra-mural department) that offers short courses for adults. For more information about universities and the courses offered, visit **www.ucas.ac.uk**.

Remaining in your current job

If you enjoy your current job, but feel that you want to develop your skills and/or improve your qualifications, there are various schemes available to help you.

Time off for training

It is possible to remain in your current job and persuade your employer to provide time off for training. From April 2011 all employees have the statutory (legal) right to request time for study or training, which is known as 'time to train'. To qualify you must be an employee of the organization and you must have worked for your employer continuously for 26 weeks before you apply. However, the following groups cannot apply for time off for training:

- agency workers;
- members of the armed forces;
- people under the compulsory school age ('school age' in Scotland);
- young people who already have a statutory right to paid time off to undertake study or training (see Chapter 5);
- young people who are 16–18 years old and already expected to take part in education or training.

To qualify for 'time to train' the training that you request must lead to a qualification and/or help you to develop skills that are relevant to your workplace, job or business. Under these rules your employer does not have to pay you a salary while you are training, nor do they have to pay your training or course fees. However, many employers agree to pay salaries and fees, especially if they believe that your training will be of benefit to their organization.

Training can take place at your workplace, at a college or training centre (see above) or could involve online learning. You can find a relevant course by using the 'course search' facility available at **https://nextstep.direct.gov.uk/ improvingyourcareerthroughlearning**. Information about how to make a request for 'time to train', including an 'application template letter', can be obtained from the employment section of **www.direct.gov.uk**. Alternatively, enter 'time to train' into the search box to be directed to the right pages.

Enrolling on an apprenticeship programme

Another option, if you are already in work and wish to remain with your employer, is to persuade your boss to enable you to begin an apprenticeship programme. Many employees begin an apprenticeship with their current employer and if you are interested in this option more information is provided in Chapter 15.

Investors in People

If your employer has Investors in People status they have made a commitment to developing the skills of the people who work for them. This means that you may be able to take advantage of education and training opportunities while you work. Speak to your employer to find out what is available. Visit **www.investorsinpeople.co.uk** for more information about Investors in People.

The Learning through Work Scheme

This scheme enables you to obtain a university-level qualification without leaving your job. It is of benefit to the organization for which you work and helps you to progress in your personal career. Learning takes place using projects you complete as part of your current working role and tutor support is provided interactively online and face-to-face. This means that all your learning takes place in the workplace and that you do not need to attend a university or college to learn. More information about this scheme can be obtained from **www.learningthroughwork.org**.

Trade union funding

In 1998 the government set up the Union Learning Fund (ULF) as a source of funding available for trade unions to help them to promote and organize learning opportunities for their members. There are a variety of schemes run by trade unions, some of which are supported by the ULF. Some of these provide free education and training for their members and/or for union representatives and officers. Others provide small grants for their members to enrol on various types of education programme. Contact your union representative for more information about what is available.

Taking part in employment training schemes

If you are currently out of work and you are finding it difficult to obtain employment (or an apprenticeship), there are a number of employment training schemes that may be of benefit. These include the following:

- New Deal is a range of programmes designed to help adults who have been out of work for long or short periods of time. Through these programmes you are given the opportunity to take part in training and work experience that is designed to help you to get back into work. If you have been unemployed for some time, ask your personal adviser about New Deal. Some of the schemes are voluntary, whereas others are compulsory.

- Employment Zones is a Jobcentre Plus programme offering long-term unemployed people help to get back to work. It is available for those on Jobseeker's Allowance, lone parents and people getting Pension Credit. At the present time it is only offered in certain parts of the UK. More advice about Employment Zones can be obtained from your Job Centre Plus personal adviser.

- The European Social Fund (ESF) is a European Union-funded programme that provides training, employment and other opportunities for people who are unemployed or have not worked for some time. To obtain help through this fund you need to be referred by your personal adviser, so contact your Jobcentre Plus adviser for more information and advice.

Another option for people who are currently out of work and who are interested in becoming an apprentice is to find a local training provider that offers apprenticeships to people who are out of work. The training organization has contacts with local companies that are willing to offer the required work placements and this could lead to full-time employment at the end of the programme. This type of scheme may not be available in all parts of the UK, so speak to your personal adviser to find out what is available in your area.

Summary

There are various education and training options available for adults who wish to improve their qualifications, skills and knowledge. This includes enrolling on courses at colleges, universities or private training organizations, on either a full-time or part-time basis. It also includes work-based learning schemes for people who wish to remain with their current employer and employment training opportunities for people who have been out of work for some time.

Once you understand all the options that are available, and if you feel that you would like to go ahead with an apprenticeship, you need to make sure that you choose the right scheme. Advice about how to do this is offered in the following chapter.

Chapter Fifteen
Finding an apprenticeship programme

Now that you have considered other options that are available to help your career progression, and if you have decided that you would like to follow the apprenticeship route, you need to make sure that you find the right programme. There are several ways that you can do this, depending on your current circumstances and interests. These include enrolling on an apprenticeship programme with your current employer, utilizing your contacts and searching for vacancies (online, through job centres, newspapers or professional associations). Once you have found an interesting vacancy you need to assess the suitability of the position and, if you decide to proceed, make an application. These issues are discussed in this chapter.

Considering apprenticeships with your current employer

Perhaps one of the easiest ways to find an apprenticeship programme is to do so with your current employer. This is a good option for people already in employment who are happy with their current employer, but who wish to train on the job and develop their skills. If you are interested in this route you should find out whether your employer already runs an apprenticeship programme and, if so, ascertain whether you qualify for the scheme. If you do qualify, making an application with a local learning/training provider should be a simple process. In most cases your employer will not require a formal application as you already work for the organization.

If your employer does not run an apprenticeship programme you can find out which local colleges and training organizations run apprenticeship programmes by using the 'learning provider' search facility available at **https://apprenticeshipvacancymatchingservice.lsc.gov.uk**. Find out whether there is a programme of interest locally and then speak to your employer to ascertain whether they will be willing to support you through the programme.

Obtaining funding

When you try to convince your employer to support you as an apprentice, you might find that you are more successful if you are able to find funding for your training. Although most funding is directed at younger apprentices (see Chapter 3), it is possible to find Adult Apprenticeship schemes that are funded or that provide grants for employers. This type of funding can come from a variety of sources, including colleges, training providers, private organizations, government and SSCs. Examples of the types of scheme that are available around the UK include the following:

- The Business and Apprenticeship Unit of Basingstoke College of Technology offers a grant to employers who are looking to hire an apprentice and/or develop their workforce. To qualify, the business must have less than 250 employees. The college has a database of young students looking for training and can provide information about, and access to, various sources of funding for businesses that are interested in the vocational development of their workforce. For more information about this scheme, visit **www.bcot.ac.uk/business/apprenticeships**.

- Howden Joinery is working with ConstructionSkills to put in place a bursary scheme for new apprentice joiners. The scheme aims to fund first-year wages for around 20 new apprentice joiners. The intention is to create new opportunities for apprentices in companies that would otherwise be unable to afford to fund apprenticeships. For more information about this scheme, visit **www.howdenjoinerygroupplc.com** and for more information about ConstructionSkills, see Appendix 4.

- Blackburn College offers 16–18 apprenticeships and Adult Apprenticeships for people who are both in and out of work. If candidates are 19+ and currently in employment, their employer could get £500 when the employee starts an apprenticeship with the college. For more information about this scheme, visit **www.blackburn.ac.uk**.

- Premier Partnership is a training provider based in Doncaster that can offer 100 per cent funded Adult Apprenticeships. There is no upper age limit and they are ideal for current employees. Training is delivered as a work-based programme and suits existing employees who wish to equip themselves with nationally recognized qualifications for the benefit of themselves and their organization. For more information about this scheme, visit **www.fundedapprenticeships.co.uk**.

Contact your local college/training provider, or the relevant SSC (see Appendix 4), to find out whether funding is available for Adult Apprenticeships in your locality and area of work.

Utilizing your contacts

As an adult it is possible that you have developed a network of useful contacts during your lifetime. This can include work colleagues, employers, family, friends, neighbours and people that you have met through a variety of social and work situations. When finding out about apprenticeships, cast your net wide as opportunities can present themselves in unexpected ways (see case study, below).

CASE STUDY

My brother has just bought a new car (it's quite an old car really) but it's new to him! When I was at my brother's house he and his mate had their heads under the bonnet trying to sort something out. It turns out his mate works in the car trade and was an apprentice himself. He told me all about what he did and how it helped him to get started as a mechanic. He knew someone who still employed apprentices and he's got contacts with bigger dealers. I've got some names of people and he said I can tell them he gave me their details. I haven't done anything yet but I think it might help my chances because sometimes people are better at helping you if they know you are a friend of a friend.

SOURCE Louise (potential car sales apprentice) Weymouth, via e-mail

In addition to utilizing your contacts it is important that you register your details with as many organizations as possible so that you can find out about new vacancies as soon as they become available. Chapter 6 provides advice about registering for free e-mail and/or text message alerts so that you can remain one step ahead of competitors.

Searching for vacancies

If you are unable to find a vacancy with your current employer or through utilizing your contacts, you need to know how to search for a suitable apprenticeship vacancy elsewhere. The following services and organizations will help you to do this (for more detailed information about each of these methods, see Chapter 6):

- online directories, databases and search facilities:
  - **https://apprenticeshipvacancymatchingservice.lsc.gov.uk** (England);
  - **www.mappit.org.uk** (Scotland);
  - **www.careerswales.com/16to19** (Wales);
  - **www.careersserviceni.com** (Northern Ireland);
- job centres and careers services:
  - **www.careers-scotland.org.uk** (Scotland);
  - **www.careerswales.com** (Wales);
  - **www.careersserviceni.com** (Northern Ireland);
  - **https://nextstep.direct.gov.uk** (England);
  - **www.direct.gov.uk/en/YoungPeople** (young people);
  - **http://jobseekers.direct.gov.uk** (jobseekers);
  - **www.direct.gov.uk/en/Employment/Jobseekers** (jobseekers);
- trade, craft and professional associations (contact the relevant association direct);
- journals and trade magazines;
  - **www.changingcareersmagazine.co.uk** (for information and advice about changing careers);
  - **www.opendoorsmedia.co.uk** (for regional training, learning and job opportunities);

- Sector Skills Councils (see Chapter 1 for more information about SSCs and Appendix 4 for contact details);
- local and national newspapers;
- apprenticeship fairs (see example, below).

CASE STUDY

As part of the research for this book I was kindly invited along to an apprenticeship fair on Monday, 7 February 2011. The fair was organized by the South West Regional Assessment Centre (SWRAC) and exhibitors included local colleges and training providers and representatives from the National Apprenticeship Service, City & Guilds and Job Centre Plus.

The fair provided the opportunity for young people and adults to find out about apprenticeships and was attended by over 700 people. SWRAC is aiming to develop their own apprenticeships in areas such as business and administration, carry and deliver goods, cleaning and support services, and team leading and management. For more information about apprenticeships with SWRAC, and to find out about future fairs, visit **www.apprenticeshipcentre.co.uk**.

Assessing the suitability of an apprenticeship

Once you have found an apprenticeship programme that is of interest, you need to make sure that it is suitable for you, personally. To do this you should take note of the following points:

1 Do you have the right skills, experience and qualifications to succeed on the programme? Is the apprenticeship at the right level to enable you to develop, personally? See Chapter 2 for information about the different levels of apprenticeship and the qualifications that are required for each level. You need to make sure that you do not overstretch yourself too much, which may cause stress and anxiety and make it hard for you to complete the programme successfully. However, you also need to make sure that the programme provides the opportunity for you to learn new skills, improve your knowledge and help with your personal development. See Chapter 7 for information about making the most of your previous experience and qualifications.

2 Are you sure that the type of apprenticeship is suitable? Is it a sector that you know a lot about, or do you need to carry out further research to find out more about this sector? See Appendix 4 for contact details of SSCs, which provide more information about apprenticeships and the work roles within specific sectors.

3 Do you know enough about what the job entails? Do you need to find out more about specific work tasks, working conditions, work colleagues and your prospective employer? Is it possible to visit the workplace to speak to other employees or apprentices? See Chapter 6 for more information about researching employers and Chapters 3 and 16 for more information about apprenticeship working conditions and contracts.

4 Do you understand what training you will need to complete? Are you happy to undertake the type of training required and do you think you will be able to cope with any independent study that you need to complete? Will family commitments affect your ability to complete the required level of training? If you have to train away from home, are you able to do so? See Chapter 3 for more information about the type of training that will be required.

5 Will you be starting the programme with other apprentices? If so, have you met any of the candidates or found out more about the type of people that apply for such positions? Do you think you will be able to work well with these people?

6 If you have financial commitments, such as a mortgage or children, is the salary enough for you to meet these commitments? If you have to take a drop in salary to become an apprentice, can you afford to do so? See Chapter 3 for more information about apprenticeship salaries.

CASE STUDY

According to EngineeringUK, there was an 88 per cent increase in the number of adult engineering apprentices (those open to people over the age of 25) between 2009 and 2010, compared to an 8 per cent decrease in young engineering apprentices (those open to people between the ages of 16 and 18) over the same period. The rise in apprentices over the age of 25 is thought to be linked to increases in funding for Adult Apprenticeships and an increased demand for retraining opportunities following the economic downturn. For more information about EngineeringUK and their research, visit **www.engineeringuk.com**.

Applying for an apprenticeship

Once you have worked your way through the questions listed above, and you believe that the apprenticeship programme you have found is suitable, you can make an application.

Application procedures vary, depending on the type of apprenticeship and the organization offering the position. Some of the online services listed above enable you to register and fill in an application form that can be adapted and sent to different employers (see Chapter 7 for information about how to do this). In other cases you will need to apply direct to the organization. Some companies will enable you to do this online, whereas others will require you to complete a paper application or send in a CV. As an adult you probably have experience of completing this type of application form and CV, but if you need any further advice about how to do this, see Chapter 7.

When applying for an apprenticeship you are likely to be more successful if you take note of the following:

- Ensure that your previous qualifications, skills and experience are suitable for the position. Make sure that you emphasize any relevant experience and qualifications that you have. If you are a jobseeker your personal adviser should be able to offer advice about this.

- All applications should be free from spelling mistakes, grammatical errors and typing mistakes. If submitting online, you may find it useful to print a copy of the form to proof-read before you submit.

- When sending any printed information, make sure that you use good quality paper and that your toner cartridge is full and does not create blotches or spots on your paper.

- Act professionally at all times. If you are contacted by prospective employers, respond as quickly as possible with politeness and courtesy.

- Make sure that you can attend all interviews, informal sessions or tests when required. Turn up promptly and don't be late.

- Dress smartly, make good eye-contact and pay attention to your body language. Sit up straight, don't slouch, don't fiddle and listen carefully to all questions.

- Answer fully and politely, making eye-contact with all interviewers.

- If you are worried about your interview technique, ask a friend or family member to carry out a mock interview with you. If you are a jobseeker, speak to your personal adviser who will be able to arrange a mock interview and/or offer further advice about how to perform well during a job interview.

More information about applying for an apprenticeship and attending interviews is provided in Chapter 7. You will also find a list of skills and traits that employers consider to be important. The more of these that you can demonstrate, the more successful you are likely to be in obtaining the position.

CASE STUDY

Apprenticeship Training Limited (ATL) is a training company for people who already work, or want to work, in the Building Services Engineering sector. Building Services covers the heating, ventilation, plumbing, gas, electrical, renewables and refrigeration and air conditioning trades. ATL offers full-time, part-time, block weeks, weekend and evening courses for adults who are thinking of changing careers, in addition to offering apprenticeship programmes. ATL have produced a guide called 'Get into Building Services', which provides information about getting trained and becoming a qualified building services professional. For more information about ATL and to download this guide, visit **www.apprenticeshiptraining.co.uk**.

Summary

As an adult you have had the chance to develop skills and build experience on which you can draw when finding and applying for an apprenticeship. However, you also need to acknowledge that family and financial commitments may constrain your choices, so careful research must be undertaken to make sure that you choose the right programme. You must be clear about what the work and training entails and make sure that you can commit to the time needed for training and study.

If you intend to apply for a place on an apprenticeship programme, it is important to understand more about what working as an apprentice will entail. These issues are discussed in the following chapter.

Chapter Sixteen
Undertaking an apprenticeship

If you are interested in obtaining a place on an apprenticeship programme, it is useful to know more about what it is like to undertake an apprenticeship. This includes gaining a clear understanding of the structure and length of the programme and knowing about the working conditions, salary and training requirements. It is also useful to take note of the personal benefits that can be gained from taking part in an apprenticeship programme and understand possible progression routes once you have completed the programme. These issues are discussed in this chapter.

Understanding the structure and length of apprenticeships

Chapter 2 provides information about the types of apprenticeship that are available in the different parts of the UK. It includes information about the structure of apprenticeships and details about the length of programmes. This information makes it clear that apprenticeship programmes can vary considerably, both in structure and length of time that they take to complete. Therefore, as an adult who may have family and financial commitments, it is important that you are fully aware of what your apprenticeship programme entails.

Most of this information should be contained within your employment contract (see below). However, if you are unclear about any clause within the contract, or if you are unsure about any aspect of your programme, you should speak to your employer or mentor to clarify the position. As we saw in Chapter 3, you should be appointed a mentor in the workplace and you will also have a trainer who is available to help with any questions that you may have about your training and the qualifications that you are taking. In addition to this, some employers realize that it is useful for apprentices to have extra support from someone who has had similar experiences and, therefore, arrange a mentoring programme amongst first- and second-year apprentices (see case study below). These mentors can be a useful source of information and can provide advice about how to rectify any problems or answer any queries that you may have.

CASE STUDY

Dorset County Council realized the importance of providing another point of contact for their apprentices. It was felt that this person should be someone that apprentices could trust and who could provide first-hand advice on all aspects of the training. Therefore, a mentoring scheme was developed to provide all new apprentices with a mentor from the second-year group.

A mentor is allocated for the duration of the mentee's apprenticeship. The matching process of the mentee with a mentor begins as soon as the new learner has been recruited. Members of staff use information provided by the learner to ensure that both learners have something in common, for example they may live in the same area or have attended the same school. Members of staff believe that this mentoring system has made the apprenticeship programme more enjoyable for apprentices in both the first and second years. For more information about apprenticeships with Dorset County Council, visit **http://jobs.dorsetforyou.com/apprenticeship**.

Knowing about employment contracts

As we saw in Chapter 3, apprentices who have worked for an employer for more than two months should receive a written statement or contract of employment. This contract should include the following:

- the names of you and your employer;
- the title of the job/apprenticeship;
- the date you started work;

- the length of the apprenticeship (which could be in terms of a specific time-scale or when a particular qualification has been achieved);
- the qualifications that are to be worked towards;
- where the apprenticeship is based, for example whether you will have to work in more than one location;
- the type of training that you are to receive and where this is to take place (eg college, day release, attending different sites of the employer);
- your salary;
- how you will be paid (eg weekly, monthly etc);
- the hours of work and the hours of your training (this should be a minimum of 30 working hours a week and at least 280 guided learning hours in the first year, which should take place during your contractual working hours; see Chapter 3);
- your holiday entitlement, which should include the number of days off per year and how much holiday pay you will receive;
- your sick pay entitlement;
- how much warning you must give the employer if you want to leave the apprenticeship;
- what the disciplinary, dismissal and grievance procedures are in the workplace;
- whether you can join the employer's occupational pension scheme, if there is one.

In addition to the express terms laid out in your contract, there are also implied terms, which are terms that are not specifically agreed between the employer and apprentice, but are based on custom, practice and agreement reached with trade unions and staff associations. These include issues such as duty of trust and duty of care, and they are discussed in detail in Chapter 3.

Apprenticeship Agreements

The government has announced its intention to introduce an Apprentice Agreement in England and Wales, which will be a contract entered into between the employer and the apprentice. It is intended that this agreement will do the following:

- Set out both the on-the-job training and the learning away from the work place that will be delivered.

- Make clear what job role an apprentice will be qualified to hold on completion.

- Stipulate the supervision that an apprentice will receive throughout the period of the apprenticeship.

At the time of writing, the introduction of this Agreement has been delayed and it is unclear when it will be implemented (see Chapter 3).

Redundancy

Although all employment contracts, by law, must include information about the amount of notice that you must be given if you are to be dismissed by your employer, this is more problematic in the case of apprenticeships. This is because apprentices have significant additional rights that are not available to other employees, especially concerning redundancy. For example, if your employer is unable to keep you on as an apprentice because of a downturn in the economy, they cannot make you redundant because this would be a breach of contract (that is, you will have been dismissed before the scheduled end of the programme).

In this case you are entitled to receive costs and benefits equivalent to that which you would have received if you had continued the apprenticeship to its conclusion and also compensation for your employer's failure to train you. It may also be possible to claim for financial loss that you may incur owing to the fact that you have not become a fully qualified tradesperson (see the legal case study in Chapter 3). If your employment contract contains a redundancy clause you should seek further advice before you sign. Visit your local Citizen's Advice Bureau in person or visit their website for help and advice: **www.adviceguide.org.uk**.

Dismissal

It is possible for an employer to dismiss you if you are in breach of your contract, for example you do not undertake the required level of training, you fail to turn up for work on a regular basis or there are problems with your conduct and behaviour. In these cases you are unlikely to be successful if you try to challenge for unfair dismissal. Despite this, you should note that your employer should provide more leeway than they would do with a normal employee.

As we saw in Chapter 1, traditionally, apprenticeship schemes set the employer in loco parentis, that is, employers took on more responsibilities and duties than they did for other employees, almost becoming substitute parents. Today, employers not only have a duty to train you, but they also have a duty to look after your personal development and growth, which includes the development of skills, helping you to mature and become a useful member of the workforce. Therefore, they should try to help and support you through problems, rather than turn immediately to dismissal. Your employer is only able to dismiss you when they are able to prove that your conduct/behaviour is so bad that it is impossible to train you and to continue with the programme.

Making a complaint

If you feel that your employer is in breach of contract or that working conditions are not as stated or are unsafe, you may decide that you need to make a complaint in the hope that the problem can be rectified. If you decide to do this you should follow the procedure outlined below:

1 Obtain a copy of your employer's grievance procedure. This could be available in your staff handbook or on your employer's intranet, for example. If you can't find a copy, speak to your mentor, trainer or human resource department. You may also find it useful to consult the ACAS Code of Practice (details below).

2 Try to solve the problem on an informal basis first. Speak to your line manager, mentor or the human resource or personnel department. Make sure that you speak to someone who is in a senior position and able to deal with the problem. Don't confront the person who may be causing the problem and keep emotions to a minimum.

3 Write down brief notes about each meeting that you have, keeping a record of what was said, by whom and when.

4 If your informal complaint is not dealt with satisfactorily you may have to start formal proceedings. If you choose to follow this route you should consult the ACAS Code of Practice for more information and to make sure that you follow the correct procedures (details below). This is important if your case should progress to an employment tribunal.

5 The first stage involves putting your complaint in writing. The grievance procedures should provide details of how to do this and information about where to send your complaint. Keep a copy of all correspondence.

6 Attend a meeting to discuss your complaint.

7 If your complaint is not dealt with satisfactorily you will need to appeal to your employer. This should be done in writing and you should explain why you are not happy with the decision.

8 Attend another meeting to discuss your appeal. You are entitled to take a colleague or trade union representative with you to the meeting, which should be attended by a more senior manager who can help to resolve the problem.

9 Receive your employer's final decision.

10 If you are still not happy, you may want to consider mediation, early conciliation or an employment tribunal. If you decide to follow any of these routes you should seek professional advice. More information and advice about these procedures can be obtained from ACAS (details below) or from your local Citizen's Advice Bureau.

Knowing about working conditions and wages

Your employment contract should include information about working conditions, including your working hours (which should be a minimum of 30 hours a week; see Chapter 3), your holiday and sick pay entitlement and information about disciplinary, dismissal and grievance procedures (see above). Some organizations also provide a staff handbook that provides all this information and also covers issues such as health and safety, stress, teamwork and opportunities for personal development. Larger companies will provide orientation/induction training that will cover working conditions, health and safety and any other aspects of the job that are deemed important.

Before you begin an apprenticeship programme a representative from your training provider will visit the workplace to check on issues such as health and safety and working conditions. As we can see from Laura's example in Appendix 3, this type of assessment will be as flexible as possible and try to help both the apprentice and employer to achieve conditions that are suitable for all concerned.

Information about how much you are to be paid and by which method should be included in your employment contract (see above). Contracts may also include information about overtime payments, but if they do not you should speak to your employer to find out how much you are to be paid if you work over your normal working hours. For information about apprentice salaries, see Chapter 3.

Undertaking learning and training

As an apprentice you will be required to undertake learning and training that will help you to gain your qualifications and successfully complete your apprenticeship. Training can take place in the workplace, or you may be expected to attend a training centre or college on day release or block release. Although training programmes vary considerably, depending on the learning/training provider, in your first year you must receive at least 280 guided learning hours, which can be 'off the job' or 'on the job' guided learning. 'Off the job' guided learning enables you to develop technical skills and theoretical knowledge and can be delivered in the workplace, in a college or on training provider premises. 'On the job' guided learning enables you to demonstrate and practise job-related skills and is delivered in the workplace and through the practical experience of doing the job.

Some larger companies that have well-established apprenticeship programmes have their own training centres and provide hotel accommodation and all meals for their apprentices while they are training. Other companies expect you to make your own way to college every week to undertake your learning. Some companies will pay travel expenses, whereas others will not. Therefore, if you have to travel a distance to undertake training, you need to make sure that you can afford to do so. Grants and bursaries may be available from local charities if you are struggling financially.

During your training you are allocated a mentor/trainer who works with you to ensure that the training is well planned and that there are no problems (see Chapter 3). If you do experience any problems, or need advice about any aspect of your training or learning, this person should be your first contact. If your training is arranged on a block release basis you are given your mentor/trainer's telephone number so that you can contact them at any time. Indeed, many companies ensure that hotels providing accommodation for apprentices have contact numbers for all mentors, trainers and programme managers. Also, each apprentice has a contact number for the person responsible for their pastoral care during training blocks (see case studies in Chapter 12). Your trainer should be able to offer advice about sources of funding (for travel and childcare, for example) if you are struggling financially.

Completing the apprenticeship successfully

You are more likely to complete your apprenticeship successfully if you take note of the following points:

- Make sure that you conduct thorough and careful research so that you choose the right programme and employer (see Chapter 6). It is easier to remain motivated and do well on the programme if you have a high level of interest in your training and learning. It is important that you feel stimulated and that you are given tasks that stretch you, whether mentally, physically or both. If you find that you are not being stretched, or that you are bored with your work or training, speak to your mentor, employer or trainer to find out whether you can train at a higher level or be given more complex work tasks.

- If you encounter any problems, deal with them as soon as possible. Speak to your line manager, mentor or trainer. Remember that other work colleagues can be a useful source of information, advice and support, so try to foster cooperation rather than competition with colleagues and other apprentices. Try to mix with colleagues where possible, perhaps on a social basis, as you will find it more enjoyable and productive in the workplace if you get on well with others.

- In order to gain your qualifications you need to make sure that you attend all training sessions and complete all the work that is required. If you are struggling with any aspect of the training, speak to your trainer as soon as possible. Meet all deadlines and hand in work on time. If you have to hand in work to specific deadlines, give yourself plenty of time to complete the work, allowing for problems such as computer crashes or family commitments. If you find that you need to improve your study skills, consult the Further reading section, below.

- Take note of the skills that you are developing and the qualifications that you gain. You will find it easier to remain motivated if you are able to recognize the personal benefits that you are gaining as a result of taking part in the apprenticeship programme. You may find it useful to keep a written record of the skills that you develop as these will be useful when you apply for jobs in the future. For a list of the type of transferable skills that you could develop, see Chapter 8.

Moving on

There are a variety of progression routes available, depending on the type and level of apprenticeship and your preferences, skills and ability. Some apprentices decide to stay with their employer and are offered a full-time position, with the possibility of further career progression within the same organization. Others decide to use their new skills and qualifications to apply for more advanced positions with a different employer or to become self-employed. (When Apprenticeship Agreements are introduced they should make it clear what job role you are qualified to hold on completion.)

It is also possible to use qualifications gained during an apprenticeship to apply for further study, which could include Advanced Apprenticeships, Higher Apprenticeships, Diplomas, foundation degrees or Bachelor's degrees (see Chapter 14).

BTEC, OCR, Key Skills and Functional Skills qualifications now have UCAS Tariff points allocated to them. This means that you can use these qualifications to help you gain points for university entry. However, you should note that the Tariff only includes qualifications recognized as Level 3 and above in England, Wales and Northern Ireland (Level 5/6 in Scotland) or equivalent. (From April 2011 Functional/Key Skills qualifications at Level 2 will be considered, as long as certain conditions are met.) Also, universities and colleges in the UCAS scheme may not consider particular qualifications to be suitable for entry to their higher education courses. Any Level 3 qualifications that do not help students progress to higher education will not attract points. For more information about UCAS Tariff, visit **www.ucas.ac.uk**.

CASE STUDY

The University of Birmingham offers Whitworth Scholarship Awards for prospective or current undergraduates or postgraduates of any engineering discipline who have completed a two-year engineering apprenticeship. The scholarships are valued up to £18,000 (for full-time study up to £4,500 per year is available over four years, for part-time study up to £3,000 per year). The closing date for applications is 30 June each year. For more information about this scheme, visit **www.whitworthscholarships.org.uk**. For more information about Birmingham University, visit **www.birmingham.ac.uk**.

Summary

Apprenticeship programmes vary in length and structure, depending on the type and level of programme, and on the organization for which you work. Salaries also vary, although the government has set in place a minimum wage that must be paid to all apprentices. Details of working conditions, holiday entitlement and sick pay are included in your employment contract, along with information about grievances and dismissal. If you have any problems during your programme you should try to rectify them as quickly as possible, on an informal basis in the first instance. As your programme progresses you should take note of the skills that you are developing as these will enable you to progress further in your chosen career.

This section of the book has provided information for people who are thinking about becoming an apprentice as a way to change career, for those seeking work and adults who are already in work and wish to embark on an apprenticeship programme with their current employer. The appendices go on to provide further information, including a list of the many different types of apprenticeship that are available, frequently asked questions, case studies and useful addresses and websites for those who need to find out more about what is available. I hope that you have enjoyed reading this book and that you find it useful. I wish you every success with finding and completing your apprenticeship programme.

Further information

www.acas.org.uk
The Advisory, Conciliation and Arbitration Service (ACAS) aims to improve organizations and working life through better employment relations. They have developed a Code of Practice for people who need to instigate grievance procedures. It sets out standards of fairness and reasonable behaviour that employers and employees are expected to follow in most situations when dealing with a dispute. Visit the website to access the Code and for more information about disputes, mediation, working contracts and salaries.

Further reading

Dawson, C (2011) *The Complete Study Skills Guide*, How to Books, Oxford

Appendix 1
The different types of apprenticeship

This appendix lists the types of apprenticeship that are available in each sector, along with examples of the job roles that are available for Level 2, Level 3 and Level 4 apprenticeships, where applicable (please note, it is not possible to list all job roles – these are examples, but there are many more available). The categories and roles are based on information supplied by the National Apprenticeship Service (NAS). Practical examples of apprenticeship schemes relevant to each sector are also provided, so that you can get an idea of the type of programme that is available.

Although the information from the NAS is relevant to schemes in England, there are similar schemes available in all parts of the UK. If you are interested in finding out more about any of the apprenticeships listed below, visit the NAS website (**www.apprenticeships.org.uk**) or the website of the relevant Sector Skills Council listed in Appendix 4.

Agriculture, horticulture and animal care

Agriculture

Level 2
general farm/agricultural worker
assistant stock person
assistant dairyperson
sheep shearer
tractor driver

Level 3
combine driver/head combine driver
stock person/dairyperson
small holder
farming technician

Animal care

Level 2

kennel worker
assistant dog groomer
pet shop assistant
junior zoo keeper
kennel/cattery assistant

Level 3

animal welfare supervisor
dog trainer
dog groomer
zoo/animal keeper
dog warden

Dry stone walling

Level 2

dry stone waller
dry stone conservator
dry stone restorer

Environmental conservation

Level 2

conservation assistant
estate worker

Level 3

conservation officer (woodland, coastal)
volunteer team manager
property/estate manager

Equine

Level 2

stud assistant
stable person
groom
trek assistant

Level 3

jockey
assistant yard manager
horse riding assistant instructor
horse dealer

Farriery

Level 3

registered farrier

Fencing

Level 2
assistant fence installer
general fence installer
fence maintenance assistant

Level 3
contracts manager
electric fence installer

Floristry

Level 2
assistant florist
flower cutter/conditioner
delivery driver
florist

Level 3
buyer
senior florist
supervisor
manager

Game and wildlife management

Level 2
ghillie (eg on a fishing or deer stalking expedition)
gun dog handler
trainee keeper
warrener
wild fowl guide

Level 3
beat keeper
gamekeeper
ghillie
single-handed keeper
wild fowl guide

Horticulture

Level 2
garden centre worker
gardener
green-keeper
grounds person

Level 3
garden designer
landscaper
landscape architect
landscape manager

Land-based service engineering

Level 2
assistant technician
technician
service technician

Level 3
managing technician
service technician
team leader

Trees and timber

Level 2	Level 3
arborist craftsman	community forester
forestry worker	arboriculturalist
forestry craftsman	tree preservation officer
	lead climber

Veterinary nursing

Level 2 and Level 3

veterinary nursing assistant and veterinary nurse

CASE STUDY

The National Trust has 15 labour teams that employ 130 skilled workers to carry out the day-to-day maintenance work that is essential for the upkeep of their properties. The teams include stonemasons, joiners, carpenters, plumbers and painters. However, 25 per cent of this workforce is due to retire within the next five years so, in order to save these skills from being lost and to have a ready source of skilled workers, the Trust has set up a new Building Skills Apprenticeship. The programme, which is aimed largely at 16–19-year-olds, will train young men and women in traditional skills including stone masonry, carpentry, joinery, lead work, plumbing, painting and decorating.

The Apprenticeship Scheme is funded by the Trust's own funds and places are offered on a three-year contract basis. Each apprentice is paid £12,000 a year and college and tuition fees are also covered (2010/11 figures). For more information about this scheme, visit **www.nationaltrustjobs.org.uk**.

Arts, media and publishing

Creative

Level 2
assistant stage manager
lighting/stage electrics
assistant sound engineer
fundraising assistant
gallery staff

Level 3
arts development officer/coordinator
stage manager
production assistant
publicity and promotion officer
customer services and visitor liaison

Creative and digital media

Level 2
production runner/assistant
broadcast assistant
editing assistant
assistant to the camera crew

Level 3
junior designer
web coordinator
photographer
production secretary

Design

Level 2
graphic design assistant
interior design assistant
product design assistant
product designer

Level 3
graphic designer
interior designer
furniture designer

Games testing

Level 2 and Level 3
games tester

Information and library services

Level 2
information assistant
library assistant
IT assistant
learning resources assistant

Level 3
information officer
senior IT assistant
senior learning resources assistant
customer liaison officer

Photo imaging for staff photographers

Level 3

staff photographer

Business, administration and law

Accounting

Level 2	**Level 3**	**Level 4**
accounts assistant	accounts clerk	accounting technician
finance assistant	credit control assistant	accountant
		(with further training)
purchase ledger clerk		

Advising on financial products

Level 3

independent financial adviser
tied financial adviser (banks, building society etc.)
multi-tied financial adviser

Business and administration

Level 2
administration assistant
junior secretary
clerical assistant

Level 3
PA/secretary
office administrator
office manager

Contact centres

Level 2
receptionist
administrator
help desk operator

Level 3
sales adviser
sales team leader or manager
customer services manager

Level 4
team manager
contact centre manager
contact centre team
   leader

Customer service

Level 2
customer services adviser
customer service assistant
customer service delivery co-ordinator

Level 3
customer services manager
customer relations officer
customer service team leader

Marketing and communication

Level 2
marketing assistant
market research interviewer
event management assistant
personal assistant

Level 3
market research executive
marketing manager
advertising account executive
public relations officer

Payroll

Level 2
payroll clerk
payroll assistant
payroll administrator

Level 3
payroll ream leader or manager
payroll supervisor
payroll manager (deputy or assistant)

Providing financial services

Level 2
customer adviser
cashier
bank and building society counter clerk

Level 3
pension administrator/adviser
investment administrator
customer service representative

Sales and telesales

Level 2
shop floor staff
call centre operative
telesales executive
customer sales adviser

Level 3
telesales professional
sales or telesales team leader
regional sales adviser
customer service team leader

Team leading and management

Level 2
team leader
section leader
charge hand

Level 3
section manager
team manager
store manager

CASE STUDY

In 2009 BT launched a customer service apprenticeship scheme for contact centre advisers. The scheme combines classroom work, one-to-one mentoring and on-the-job training and leads to a BTEC in Customer Service, an NVQ and Key Skills in Literacy and Numeracy certificate. There is also the opportunity to take the Advanced Apprenticeship in Customer Service, which is a two-year programme working towards an NVQ Level 3 and the Higher Apprenticeship in Contact Centre Management, which is a three-year programme working towards an NVQ Level 4. It is also possible to work towards a foundation degree in customer service and contact centre management.

Pay ranges are based on individual roles and are reviewed annually. The current range is £10,000 to £15,000 a year (2011 figures). Apprentices receive the usual benefits that are offered to all employees, including 25 days' holiday a year, opportunities to buy BT shares, the option to join the company pension scheme and staff discounts on BT products, including free BT Broadband/Talk & Vision Package. More information about becoming an apprentice with BT can be obtained from **www.bt4me.co.uk** and **www.btplc.com/careercentre**.

Construction, planning and the built environment

Building services engineers

Level 3
project designer
project manager
financial manager/budget controller

Construction

Level 2	Level 3
joiner	civil engineering technician
roofer	construction operative
bricklayer	project designer
painter and decorator	

Electrical and electronic servicing

Level 2
television receiver and aerial installer

domestic appliance installer
servicing, maintenance and repair work

Level 3
high technology installation, service, repairs

Electrotechnical

Level 3
electrical machine technician
installation electrician
maintenance electrician
highway systems electrician

Heating, ventilating, air conditioning and refrigeration

Level 2 and Level 3
welder
ductwork installer
refrigeration and air condition technician
service and maintenance engineer
heating and ventilation fitter

Plumbing

Level 2 and Level 3
plumber

Set crafts

Level 3
carpenters, painters and plasterers for the arts and entertainment industry

Surveying

Level 3
building surveyor
quantity surveyor
valuation surveyor

CASE STUDY

Lovell is a company that builds and refurbishes social housing across the UK. It has over 1,500 employees and refurbishes over 18,000 homes each year. Apprenticeships are available in bricklaying, carpentry, painting and decorating, and maintenance operations. Learning for the apprenticeship takes place in eight one-week residential blocks at the Lovell Craft Academy. All learning is fully funded and Lovell pays all costs associated with residential stay at the Academy, including travel expenses. Apprentices join a two-year programme and can expect to complete their NVQ Level 2 in 18 months. They can then practise their skills at work before deciding whether to move on to an apprenticeship at NVQ Level 3.

All apprentices are given a toolkit, personal protective equipment and help with obtaining their Construction Skills Certification Scheme (CSCS) card (a card that provides proof of occupational competence). For more information about the Lovell apprenticeship scheme, visit **www.lovell.co.uk** and for more information about CSCS cards, visit **www.cscs.uk.com**.

Education and training

Learning and development

Level 3
trainer
training and development office
human resource professional

Supporting teaching and learning in schools

Level 2 and Level 3
teaching assistant
classroom assistant
learning support assistant
special needs assistant
behaviour support assistant
bilingual support assistant

CASE STUDY

West Nottinghamshire College offers an Apprenticeship Level 2 Certificate in Supporting Teaching and Learning in Schools, which is aimed at people who are already employed within a school environment. The certificate usually takes between 18 months and two years to complete. It is free for people between the ages of 16 and 18 and employers pay the fee for people who are above this age. During the apprenticeship the employer is obliged to pay at least the minimum rate for an apprentice.

The apprenticeship focuses on providing support in the classroom under the direction of a teacher, and enables apprentices to develop their working knowledge and understanding of how to promote the development of children and enable them to achieve their full potential. Apprentices learn about legislative guidelines, policies and curriculum requirements, and develop their numeracy, literacy and information technology skills to help them to carry out their work more effectively and efficiently. For more information about this scheme, visit **www.wnc.ac.uk**.

Engineering and manufacturing technologies

Building products occupations

Level 2 and Level 3
delivery driver
production operative
precast concrete installer
crane operator

Ceramics manufacturing

Level 2 and Level 3
ceramic maker
decorator

Coating operations (manufacture and production of coatings for items such as walls, cars, computers and coats)

Level 2 and Level 3
quality control operative
maintenance engineer
production operative

Driving goods vehicles

Level 2 and Level 3
LGV driver

Electricity industry

Level 2 and Level 3
Installers, operators and technicians for power stations and the National Grid

Engineering

Level 2

aero engine component assembly

automotive instrument repairer
avionics instrument calibration technician
CAD operator
CNC operator

motorsport technician
vehicle body repair technician
welder

Level 3

manufacturing maintenance
   engineer
watchmaker/clockmaker
maintenance welder (skilled)
aircraft service engineer
specialist vehicle
   maintenance engineer
repair and overhaul engineer

Engineering construction

Level 2 and Level 3

steel erector
rigger
welder
pipefitter
mechanical fitter
electrical fitter
project controller

Engineering technology

Level 4

maintenance engineering technician
electrical engineering technician
aerospace engineering technician

Extractive and mineral processing operations

Level 2

maintenance engineers (junior)
processing plant operator
driller
highway maintenance workers
road building workers

Level 3

supervisor of processing plant
construction supervisor
laboratory or field technician
site, quarry or operations supervisors
road construction supervisor

Food manufacture

Level 2 and Level 3

baker
brewer
butcher
fishmonger
logistics controller
meat process worker
quality controller
food scientist/technician

Furniture, furnishings and interiors manufacturing industry

Level 2 and Level 3

garden and leisure furniture designer and manufacturer
soft furnishings designer, manufacturer or installer
furniture restorer, designer, manufacturer or installer
kitchen and bedroom designer or installer
office and contract furniture assembler
restorer, repairer, polisher

Gas industry

Level 2 and Level 3

trainee gas service engineer
trainee gas distribution technician
trainee emergency service engineer

Glass industry occupations

Level 2	Level 3
windscreen fitter and repairer	glazier and installer
glass installer or fitter	glazing systems maintainer
roofline installer	automotive glazier
glass maker or manufacturer	glass processor
fabricator	fabricator
frame-maker	frame-maker

Industrial applications

Level 2 and Level 3
electrical/electronic product assembler
vehicles and metal goods assembler
marine craft assembler
aerospace assembler
metal working and machine operative
inspector and tester

Laboratory technicians

All levels
laboratory technician

Marine industry

Level 2 and Level 3
boat builder
laminator
carpenter
marine electrician
marine engineer

Metal processing

Level 2	**Level 3**
metals handler	structural steelwork fabricator
testing technician	laboratory and testing technician
production processor	materials scheduler and producer
service centre operator	team leader

Nuclear decommissioning

Level 3
decommissioning technician
laboratory technician
process technician

Paper and board manufacturing

Level 2 and Level 3
maintenance engineer

process operator

process engineer

team leader or manager

Passenger carrying vehicle driving: bus and coach

Level 2
PCV (passenger carrying vehicles) driver

Polymer processing operations

Level 2 and Level 3
sign-maker or installer

process operative

finishing and assembly operative

polymer engineer

production technician

supervisor or manager

Print and printed packaging

Level 2
machine operator (folding, binding, guillotine)

plate-maker

digital print producer

desktop publisher

graphic designer

print designer

Level 3
scanning or proofing technician

desktop publisher

graphic designer

print designer

account manager

estimator or costing clerk

Process technology

Level 2 and Level 3
chemical, pharmaceutical or petroleum industries: process operative
maintenance engineer
laboratory assistant or technician
oil and gas industry: offshore process operator or technician
offshore engineering maintenance technician

Rail transport engineering

Level 2
electrification and plant worker
track maintenance worker
traction and rolling stock worker

Level 3
communication engineering technician
signals engineering technician
electrification engineering technician

Rail transport operations

Level 2 and Level 3
train driver
signal operator
control room operator
station announcer
ticket examiner
guard
conductor
steward
travel consultant
call centre adviser

Retail motor industry: roadside assistance and recovery

Level 2
vehicle removal technician

Level 3
vehicle removal technician and
roadside technician

Retail motor industry: vehicle body and paint operations

Level 2 and Level 3
body repair technician
body finishing technician
electrical and trim technician
mechanic

Retail motor industry: vehicle fitting

Level 2 and Level 3
motor vehicle fitter (eg cars, tractors, trucks)
fast-fit technician (eg tyres, batteries, exhausts)

Retail motor industry: vehicle maintenance and repair

Level 2 and Level 3
auto electrician
vehicle technician (maintenance, diagnosis and repairs)

Retail motor industry: vehicle parts operation

Level 2 and Level 3
customer services adviser
parts adviser
vehicle parts operative (ordering, keeping records, managing returns etc)

Sea fishing

Level 2 and Level 3
deckhand
fish farmer
coastguard watch assistant or officer
merchant navy rating
royal navy rating

Sign-making

Level 2 and Level 3
sign-maker
sign designer
sign installer
quality technician
manufacturing technician

Specialized process operations (nuclear)

Level 2 and Level 3
radiation monitor
decommissioning operative
process operative
team supervisor or manager

Traffic office

Level 2 and Level 3
traffic officer (haulage or courier company)
transport manager
team supervisor or manager

Transport engineering and maintenance

Level 2 and Level 3
PCV technician
auto mechanic
auto electrician
bodywork repairer

Water industry

Level 2 and Level 3
pipe installer
pipe maintainer and repairer
plant operator
mains and services supervisor

CASE STUDY

Carnegie College in Fife is working to develop the first bespoke range of Modern Apprenticeship technician programmes for on- and off-shore wind, working in partnership with Scottish & Southern Energy, Siemens and the Sector Skills Council for Energy and Utility. It has been predicted that there is potential for up to 50,000 new jobs in the offshore wind energy sector and this type of apprenticeship scheme will help to train people in the necessary skills and provide relevant qualifications required for such expansion. For more information about Carnegie College, visit **www.carnegiecollege.ac.uk**.

Health, public services and care

Advice and guidance

Level 2	Level 3
library assistant	doctor/dental receptionist
customer services	benefits adviser
support worker	young person adviser
clerical officer	employment adviser
school secretary	learning disability support worker
help-line adviser	schools liaison officer

Children's care, learning and development

Level 2	Level 3
playgroup assistant	child-minder
nursery assistant	nursery nurse
playgroup leader	

Community development

Level 2 and Level 3

community development work

Community justice

Level 3
community safety project worker
probation service officer
youth offending team worker
substance misuse worker
prison substance misuse worker (CARAT (counselling, assessment, referral, advice and throughcare) worker)

Dental nursing

Level 3
dental nurse in a surgery, hospital, community or armed forces

Emergency fire service operations

Level 3
fire fighter for a local authority, airport, chemical works, military base or power station

Health and social care

Level 2	Level 3
nursing assistant	occupational or physiotherapy therapy assistant
care worker	radiotherapy assistant
healthcare assistant	day care manager
home care assistant	senior healthcare assistant
support worker	senior support worker

Housing

Level 2	Level 3
administrative officer	housing advice worker
housing assistant	rent officer
customer service officer	sheltered housing officer
hostel support worker	
regeneration officer	

Optical

Level 2 and Level 3
dispensing assistant
optical assistant
receptionist
assistant optician
assistant optometrist

Pharmacy technicians and assistants

Level 2 and Level 3
dispensing and pharmacy assistant
pharmacy technician

Providing security services

Level 2 and Level 3
static and patrol guard
uniformed retail security guard
store detective
CCTV operator
dog handler
private investigator

Security systems

Level 2 and Level 3
security, emergency and alarm systems installer, maintainer and/or
   engineer

Youth work

Level 2 and Level 3
youth support work
assistant youth worker

CASE STUDY

The NHS offers a wide variety of apprenticeships for people who are interested in looking for a job that enables them to carry on learning, and for those already in employment who want to gain further qualifications. Apprenticeships within the NHS are available in Scotland, Wales, Northern Ireland and England and are offered by individual NHS employers (such as trusts and health authorities). They are open to all age groups (above 16 years) and are available in many different types of work, which are grouped into occupational sectors.

Although there is no set rate of pay for apprentices, all will receive at least the National Minimum Wage for apprentices. Also, they will usually receive the same benefits as other employees such as pension contributions, subsidized canteen and leisure facilities (if available). Apprenticeships take between one and four years to complete, depending on the type of framework/programme. The length of time taken depends on the ability of the individual apprentice and the employer's requirements. For more information about apprenticeships with the NHS, visit **www.nhscareers.nhs.uk**.

Information and communication technology

IT and telecoms professionals

Level 2 and Level 3
web designer
business analyst
software developer
IT trainer and/or adviser
system support engineer or technician
aerial rigger
network planner and/or manager

IT users

Level 2 and Level 3
anyone who needs to use a computer for their job

ICT professionals

Level 3 and Level 4

web designer
business analyst
help desk operator
software developer
technical author
system support engineer
IT security
IT manager and/or team leader

CASE STUDY

Virgin Media has set up a 'Digital Heroes Apprenticeship Scheme' that offers two types of scheme: the Young Apprenticeship (12 month scheme) and the Advanced Apprenticeship: Civils and Planning (18 month scheme). Young apprentices work towards Level 2 in Communications Technology and advanced apprentices work towards Level 3 in Communications Technology. Both groups also develop their Key Skills and learn how to work in groups and on their own. To take part in the Young Apprenticeship scheme you must be between the ages of 16 and 19 in Scotland and 16 and 18 in England, and to take part in the advanced scheme you must be between the ages of 18 and 24. Apprentices will be given the opportunity to experience a variety of working environments and locations during their apprenticeship.

Young apprentices will be paid £12,000, rising to £18,350 on successful completion of their National Qualification. Advanced apprentices will be paid £17,000, with incremental salary reviews on achievement during the 18-month scheme (2011 figures). Benefits include discounts on Virgin products and half price on fixed line, broadband and digital TV services for those living in a serviceable area. For more information about this apprenticeship scheme, visit **http://careers.virginmedia.com**.

Leisure, travel and tourism

Active leisure and learning

Level 2 and Level 3

leisure and theme park attendant
sports and leisure assistant or manager
trainee psychologist
trainee physiotherapist
assistant youth and community worker
sports player
sports coach, instructor and official
fitness instructor
gardener and grounds person
playgroup leader and assistant

Aviation operations on the ground

Level 2 and Level 3

check-in staff
customer service agent
baggage handler
airfield inspector and/or maintenance worker

Cabin crew

Level 2
air cabin crew member

Sporting excellence

Level 3 (for talented athletes aged 16–18). It is available for:

- full-time contracted apprentices at professional clubs;
- full-time elite athletes receiving support from the lottery world class programme and identified by their respective national governing body (eg UK Athletics);
- young people involved in the Talented Athlete Scholarship Scheme (TASS);

- talented young people in the 'academy environment' at professional clubs not yet offered full-time terms.

Travel and tourism services

Level 2 and Level 3
travel consultant for business or leisure
team leader or manager

CASE STUDY

TUI Travel PLC was established in 2007 with the merger of First Choice Holidays PLC and the Tourism Division of TUI AG. Today the company offers an Apprenticeship in Travel Services for people interested in jobs such as travel advisers, cabin crew and call centre advisers.

Applicants need to be at least 16 years of age and must be able to work shop opening hours (including weekend work). They also must not already hold a higher education degree and will need to pass a literacy and numeracy test as part of the application. The programme takes one–two years to complete, depending on the level. On-the-job training is provided, along with a permanent contract offering a starting salary of £120 per week plus commission (2011 figures). For more information about this apprenticeship scheme, visit **www.tuitraveljobs.co.uk**.

Retail and commercial enterprise

Barbering

Level 2 and Level 3
barber

Beauty therapy

Level 2
junior beauty therapist
skin care adviser
make-up consultant
electrolysist (hair removal)

Level 3
make-up artist
masseur
beauty therapist

Carry and deliver goods

Level 2
courier
delivery van driver
dispatch rider

Cleaning and support services

Level 2 and Level 3
street cleaner (mechanized)
window cleaner
caretaker
cleaning team supervisor or manager
specialized cleaner (eg electronic equipment, high-risk areas etc)

Facilities management

Level 3
assistant facilities manager
facilities manager

Fashion and textiles

Level 2 and Level 3
grader
designer
finisher
machinist
inspector/quality controller
packer
specialist craftsperson
supervisor or manager

Hairdressing

Level 2 and Level 3
salon junior
junior stylist
hairdresser

Hospitality and catering

Level 2

waiter

silver service waiter

bar-person

cellar-person

receptionist

housekeeper

supervisor (eg youth hostels
   or small hotels)

Level 3

sous chef

head chef

head housekeeper

head of reception

manager (eg hotel or catering company)

regional manager (eg pub chain)

Logistics operations management

Level 3

logistics manager

warehouse manager

distribution manager

Mail services

Level 2 and Level 3

postman/woman

delivery driver

mail sorter

customer service representative

supervisor or manager

Nail services

Level 2

junior nail technician

sales representative

designer

session and photographic nail artist

salon manager

Level 3

nail technician

Property services

Level 2 and Level 3

estate agent
letting agent
customer service adviser
property manager

Purchasing and supply management

Level 2, Level 3 and Level 4

supply chain operator
supply chain manager
purchasing clerk
team supervisor
purchasing manager

Retail

Level 2

sales assistant
fresh food counter assistant
customer service assistant
stockroom assistant
beauty consultant
personal shopper
manager, supervisor or team leader

Level 3

senior sales assistant
baker
butcher
fishmonger
greengrocer

Retail motor industry: vehicle sales

Level 2 and Level 3

car salesperson

Spa therapy

Level 3

spa therapist

Warehousing and storage

Level 2
forklift driver
warehouse worker
specialist machine operator

CASE STUDY

Yorkshire College of Beauty Therapy offers Apprenticeships and Advanced Apprenticeships in Beauty Therapy. The courses cover topics such as beauty, massage, facial and electrotherapy, anatomy and physiology, figure diagnosis, electrolysis, aromatherapy, business studies, advertising, professional ethics, public relations, salon safety, health and hygiene, first aid and cosmetic science. The courses are open to applicants between 16 and 18, although a small number of Adult Apprenticeships are also available.

Learners are paid directly by the salons that employ them, which provide work experience while the apprentice is training. Apprentices spend one day a week at college and four days (32 hours) with their employer. The college has a large bank of salons that work in partnership with it, so placements can be found if a learner has been unable to secure their own place with an employer. For more information about this apprenticeship scheme, visit **www.ycob.co.uk**.

Appendix 2
Frequently asked questions

Q. How do I know whether an apprenticeship is the right choice for me?

A. Through undertaking careful research and by seeking professional advice. If you are a student or adult learner, see Chapter 4 and if you are a career changer, in employment or a jobseeker, see Chapter 13. You might also find it useful to read Michael's case study in Appendix 3, as he was able to receive very good information and advice.

Q. How do I find an apprenticeship programme?

A. There are various ways, including online databases, job centres, careers centres, newspapers, journals, professional associations and Sector Skills Councils. See Chapter 6 for information about all these methods.

Q. I am not young. Are there apprenticeships available for older people?

A. Yes. Adult Apprenticeships are available for people over the age of 25. Unfortunately, funding is not always available for people over this age, so you may be required to pay for training yourself. However, some employers will meet training costs for you. Also, there are additional sources of funding available for older apprentices. See Chapter 13 for more information about age-related issues.

Q. Can I do an apprenticeship with my current employer?

A. Yes, if you can convince your employer that it is a good idea and that it will be of benefit to both you and the company. For information about how to go about doing this, see Chapter 15.

Q. Can I start an apprenticeship even if I haven't got a job?

A. Yes, although this may depend on where you live in the UK and your age. Read Chapter 2 to find out what types of apprenticeship are available in the different parts of the UK. You can also find out which local colleges and organizations run apprenticeship programmes by using the 'learning provider' search facility available at **https://apprenticeshipvacancy-matchingservice.lsc.gov.uk**. Find out whether there is a programme of interest locally and contact the college/trainer direct to find out whether you can enrol on a programme even if you haven't got a job. Some colleges and training providers work closely with local employers and will sort out a work placement for you, but there may be age restrictions placed on these programmes.

Q. My parents want me to go to university, but I want to do an apprenticeship instead. How do I convince them that this is a good idea?

A. Seek professional advice and guidance to make sure that you are making the right choice. If you are certain that this is the right choice for you, ask your parents to read Section 3 of this book. Some parents don't understand the modern-day apprenticeship scheme, but once they do they may be more convinced of its merits. Also, university tuition fees are due to rise up to a maximum of £9,000 per annum from 2012 (in England). Although you can take out a student loan to cover fees and living expenses, you need to let your parents know that you would rather not be in debt for most of your working life. Read Laura's case study in Appendix 3 as this might be of interest to you.

Q. How do I apply for an apprenticeship?

A. Application procedures vary depending on the type of apprenticeship and the organization offering the position. For more information about making an application if you are a student or adult learner, see Chapter 7. If you are seeking work or changing careers, see Chapter 15.

Q. How much will I be paid?

A. You will be paid a National Minimum Wage (NMW) of £2.60 per hour if you are aged under 19 or aged 19 or over in the first year of your apprenticeship. Employers can pay above this amount, if they wish. All apprentices over the age of 19 who have completed the first year of their apprenticeship are entitled to the NMW appropriate for their age (£6.08 for workers aged 21 and over and £4.98 for workers aged 18–20 in 2011). For more information about apprenticeship salaries, see Chapter 3.

Q. Can I be made redundant if I become an apprentice?

A. Apprentices have significant additional rights that are not available to other employees, especially concerning redundancy. For example, if your employer is unable to keep you on as apprentice because of a downturn in the economy, they cannot make you redundant because this would be a breach of contract (that is, you will have been dismissed before the scheduled end of the programme). If this were to happen you are entitled to receive costs and benefits equivalent to that which you would have received if you had continued the apprenticeship to its conclusion and also compensation for your employer's failure to train you. See Chapter 16 for more information about redundancy issues.

Q. Can I be dismissed from my apprenticeship?

A. You can only be dismissed if you are in breach of the contract, for example you do not undertake the required level of training, you fail to turn up for work on a regular basis or there are problems with your conduct and behaviour. In these cases you are unlikely to be successful if you try to challenge for unfair dismissal. Despite this, you should note that your employer should provide more leeway than they would do with other employees. See Chapter 16 for more information about dismissal issues.

Q. What can I do after an apprenticeship?

A. There are various options available. For example, you could choose to continue to a higher-level apprenticeship, you could go on to university, or you could obtain a full-time job with your current employer or move on to another employer. More information about the various types of progression route for students and adult learners is provided in Chapter 9 and more information about progression routes for jobseekers and career changers is provide in Chapter 16.

Appendix 3
Case studies

Case study 1: Michael Doucas, Youth Work Apprentice, Children's Services

I met Michael on a sunny autumn day outside the Abbey in the small market town of Sherborne in North West Dorset. We sat on a bench in the Abbey grounds to discuss his apprenticeship, which was with the Children's Services section of Dorset County Council.

Michael worked at Dorchester Youth Centre for 30 hours a week and had each Thursday off work for training. He was working towards an NVQ and VRQ (Vocationally Related Qualification) Level 1 and believed that it would take him 16 to 18 months to complete. When we met he had already completed three months and three weeks of his apprenticeship and was enjoying the work, which he described in the following way:

> It's good. I do some admin work and work with young mums and their children. Yeah, it's good. We had an inflatable yesterday, a bouncy castle. It was great... We just socialize and work behind the coffee bar and then after you make some posters and do some admin work. It's all to get me involved slowly. I think it will probably get harder... We also do paperwork, like planning trips, organizing how we're getting there, like buses and trains and hotels and that.

Michael was 18 years old. He had left school in 2008 and had been unsure about what he wanted to do. First he went to college to study business administration and retail, and then he went on to 'The Rendezvous' to brush up on his English skills. It was here that he had received advice about the apprenticeship and was encouraged to apply.

I met the centre manager, Ingrid Trill, in January 2011 to find out more about the organization. The Rendezvous is officially known as Youth Resource Services (The Rendezvous, Sherborne). It was established in 1998 in response to requests from young people who had outgrown the local youth centre and who wanted somewhere to meet where they could be treated as adults. Local people, the police and West Dorset District Council all got together to raise money and to find a suitable location. Initially, this was difficult because a place was needed in the town centre where the young people tended to congregate. However, the Cheap Street Church came up with the idea of using the crypt, which, although derelict, was perfectly located on the main street in the town centre. Money was raised, the crypt refurbished and the centre opened to offer information, advice and guidance to young people, training for young people and adults and an informal drop-in centre for young people to meet. Ingrid described their work with young people in the following way:

> It's all about helping these young people; our main concern is getting these young people out of this rut where they feel they've got such low self-esteem because they've not achieved in school and that they are worthless and that they can't do any jobs and they become demotivated... They become totally unfocused and would appear to become a lost cause to parents and everybody else. We drag them out of that, build up their self-esteem, get them some qualifications which they feel then that they've achieved and then we get them work experience and then ultimately, like we've done with Michael, getting an apprenticeship or even into employment.

Michael was very pleased with the help and advice he had received at The Rendezvous. In particular, this was because he hadn't heard about apprenticeships prior to receiving this advice, and because he felt that he was well suited to the apprenticeship. He was proud of the fact that he had done well in the interview, which, he felt, had enabled him to obtain the best apprenticeship place:

> They wanted me there because Dorchester Youth Centre is the best. It's more organized than all the other ones. I've been talking to other apprentices, there's 12 when we meet up on a Thursday, and they say they haven't hardly done anything, they've done a bit of admin, going to other youth clubs but not much, so compared to mine, they love mine. That's why they put me there because I got a high score, I think.

For Michael, careers advice at school had been totally inadequate. However, the advice offered at The Rendezvous had been completely different. Ingrid believed this was because:

> We talk to the young people, we give them the time, we treat them as individuals, we pursue all options and we've got a lot of knowledge about what careers and opportunities are out there.

After my meeting with Ingrid I spoke to another member of The Rendezvous staff, Petra. She agreed with Ingrid and offered further insight into why the centre was able to help Michael and other young people:

We tend to do reviews all the way through the programme while they are with us and apprenticeships are one of the things that we might talk about during the review. A lot of them come in not knowing what they want to do, so we are trying to focus them, think about what you want to do when you leave us. What are you going to progress on to and all that advice and guidance is ongoing throughout the programme. So Michael, when he started with us, for example, wasn't too clear about where he wanted to go. Eventually it turned out that possibly youth work and then what happens is that while they are on programme we are always looking for opportunities for them to apply for. Luckily this apprenticeship came up while Michael was still on the programme. So we help them apply for either jobs, college, apprenticeships, all that sort of thing. And try and give them qualifications that will help them get into the apprenticeship that they have chosen, and then if they want support once they've left us we're here to help them with that as well.

The only problem that Michael had encountered during his apprenticeship was to do with travel expenses. He lived in Sherborne but worked in Dorchester, which is located about 20 miles away, as he explained:

You should be getting paid travel I reckon. 'Cos I don't get travel all the way from Sherborne to Dorchester, even though I'm supposed to get it for Thursdays but I can't because my training centre is actually in Dorchester and that's my workplace as well so I can't get it... It's weird. But it's going to be sorted because they wouldn't give it to me and then they will... My mum takes me in the mornings which she wants petrol money for, and I go back on a bus, but it goes all the way around the villages.

Petra believed that this was a real problem for young people living locally and that this reduced the options available for jobs and careers:

Well again you see if the apprenticeships aren't out there and if you are talking about young people from this area and you say well there are lots of apprenticeships in Bristol, well how are they going to get there? They're not going to live there because they can't afford to do that, so there might be lots of opportunities in cities, which is fine if you live in that city... So trying to get them into apprenticeships, if the employers aren't coming on board there is absolutely nothing we can do.

Ingrid agreed that apprenticeships were not available in the local area and that this made it difficult for the young people of Sherborne to obtain places on apprenticeship programmes:

No, they're just not out there. There's very few in Sherborne, if any, most would be I guess Yeovil or Dorchester or Bournemouth or beyond, in which case, how do these kids get there? Seventeen or 18, if they don't drive themselves how do they get there? Public transport wouldn't get them there. The fare to Yeovil is about £6.80, they couldn't afford that on an apprenticeship daily.

Michael was paid £150 a week, which he considered to be 'fine' because he could afford to live on that amount. Although travel expenses were causing him a problem when we met, he felt that the problem would be rectified in the near future.

When asked what advice Michael would give to his friends about choosing a job or career, he said that he would tell them to go to The Rendezvous and 'take it from there'. Although Michael was not sure about what he wanted to do after he has finished his apprenticeship, he thought that it might be 'something to do with counselling' and he felt that his apprenticeship would be a useful stepping stone to achieving this. He reported that he returned to The Rendezvous on a regular basis and members of staff were happy to offer help and advice when required.

Case study 2: Laura Culshaw, Business and Administration Apprentice

I met Laura on a winter morning in Starbucks, Weymouth. Laura was a business and administration apprentice, working for an employer based just outside Weymouth. When Laura was studying at sixth form she had decided that an apprenticeship would be the right route for her, partly because her dad had been an apprentice and had been able to offer useful advice:

> At school nothing was touched upon about apprenticeships or work, it was all go to university. My dad was an apprentice, he's a welder, so he was an apprentice since he was 17, so I asked him about the whole apprenticeship scheme. Although it's changed it gave me an insight. I got more information from him than anyone else so I was determined that I was going to do an apprenticeship.

Her parents had been incredibly supportive and were willing to support Laura in whatever career path she chose. They were also happy to support her as an apprentice:

> They both said whatever you want to do, whatever makes you happy. They are really supportive of me now because I'm still living at home and I only get my apprenticeship wage. They really supported me and encouraged me to do well. I'm running for apprentice of the year with the *Dorset Echo*, so my mum's ringing all her friends, vote for Laura, so that's quite embarrassing.

Despite lack of guidance at school Laura persevered with her desire to become an apprentice, supported by her parents. She found out about the National Apprenticeship Service website and signed up. Then she applied for relevant vacancies. However, she was soon to find out that there was a problem with her age and with funding for apprenticeships:

> I applied for an apprenticeship with Wessex FM for an admin assistant and I had an interview with the college and they basically told me I was too old. That was their words, they said I'm really sorry but you're too old to do this apprenticeship and I was like sorry, I'm too old, I'm 19 next week and they were like no, sorry, no explanation, no nothing. I had no idea what it was about. My confidence was so rocked by that because I thought how can I be too old to be an apprentice? So I went to the local youth advice centre and they investigated it further and it's to do with the government and the funding. Someone there got in touch with Wessex FM and said this girl is really upset about the way that she was told she was too old to do an apprenticeship. So they said to me do you want to come and do some work experience? So I went for two weeks this time last year actually and I did some voluntary work with them and learnt all about radio which was really interesting but I still wasn't able to do an apprenticeship with them.

Laura applied for some more apprenticeships but didn't hear anything back about her applications. In desperation she decided to apply for university and was offered a place for the following year. However, at the same time she had also applied for a position with a local marketing agency. Although the funding issue was still a problem, Laura felt that gaining work experience in a marketing environment was the best route to take, so she decided to work without receiving a wage:

> At the interview she said you're over 18 so we have a problem, and I said oh, what is that, and she said well the government doesn't supply funding for over-18s as easily. So I said, OK I'll do it for free because I really wanted the experience, I wanted to do it, I'd never done anything in marketing before and I really wanted to go out there.

Laura continued with her part-time job at Debenhams so that she could get some money coming in. However, she soon found that holding down two jobs was too much for her:

> I was still working at Debenhams and was doing six days a week and five were unpaid. So it really took its toll on me and I was really exhausted and I just couldn't do it any more. So although I had a great experience there and I'm still friends with the girls I worked with, although I really loved working there I just couldn't do it so I decided to hand in my notice.

As the interview progressed, Laura also pointed out that her employer had promised to take her on as a full-time paid employee after six months, but that this position hadn't materialized. This, along with other funding issues, had helped with her decision to leave:

They said to me once I finished my unpaid placement they would take me on paid, but it got to the month when they said they were going to do that and nothing happened, that was another reason why I left. I worked it out and said well if I'm commuting to Poole there and back every day and I'm only earning this amount this isn't worth my while doing it, so that was another reason why I chose to leave. But they wouldn't have paid me extra travel expenses over the top of my wages.

Even though she had been working for the company for free, Laura was made to feel guilty that she had decided to hand in her notice and was told that she was leaving the company in the lurch. This was despite the fact that the employer had not provided the promised full-time position. Even so, Laura did not regret her decision to take on an unpaid position:

I think if your heart's in it then do it, if you're committed to doing it then go for it. But there comes a point when somebody will probably take advantage of that, which I was getting the sense of that, because they were asking more of me and they were asking me to take work home and it just got a bit too much. But I mean you've got to start somewhere. And I built up the experience in those six months. It was definitely worth doing, it was a tough six months and it just completely physically and emotionally drained me, but yes, I think it was important.

After having handed in her notice, Laura was able to find another position that suited her much better, especially as it was local and paid:

And that was when I met Julie from Popcorn Marketing. I've known her a couple of years because my mum used to work with her years ago... so I gave her a call and she said she was looking for an apprentice. So I said yes, I've done marketing unpaid for six months and she said do you want to come around so I had an informal interview with her. She has two companies. One is Extra Mile Chauffeur Travel which is based from the home. They have a fleet of five cars and they do airport transfers, weddings and they've got a minibus coach, so I do all the bookings and everything like that. And then also I work for Popcorn Marketing which is more of a consultancy. The other place I worked for was an agency, so it was completely different. Although it was marketing it was two different aspects of it.

When college staff came to speak to the new employers and check out the work premises, there were some initial problems owing to the nature of the workplace and the type of apprenticeship offered. However, the college staff and new employers were able to make suitable arrangements:

Julie and Mick work from home so members of staff at the college have never encountered that before. When I first started I was in Julie's living room because Julie worked from her house and we were in the dining room area and we had the computer and all the files, so it was quite strange for college staff because they've never had that concept. All their employers have been in a major corporate workplace, they've never actually had somebody work from home. And the other thing that was different as well was because I worked for two employers, so my wages were split between Popcorn and Extra Mile so that was something that they had never come across before, an employer that had two businesses and wanted an apprentice for them both. Although that was foreign to the college we made it work.

Laura was very happy in her new position. The only problem that she had encountered, again, was to do with funding, but she believed that this would be sorted out in the near future:

If you're 18, the way that we've been told is that you have to pay 50 per cent of your tuition fees, so Julie will come up with half and the government will come up with half. But the provider we were going through withdrew our application and said we're not entitled to funding. That's what happened a couple of weeks ago actually and we were a bit shocked, I was like well I've been doing this since November so why has this suddenly come up? We thought it was all sorted and paid for but they've withdrawn it for some reason. But we got in touch with the National Apprenticeship Service and they're searching for alternative ways to fund it. But that was quite a shock actually to Julie as well, because it just came out of the blue and it's a constant battle with funding which I think is really wrong.

Laura would like to remain in her current job because she enjoys the work and finds her employers very supportive:

I'm actually really happy where I am. I know most people use apprenticeships to either work their way up in a company or to leap between jobs and companies and such, but it's only me who works there with Julie and her husband so it's quite nice, it's a secluded environment. They work from home, I do their marketing, I work for Extra Mile. In a way it's perfect because when I'm working for Extra Mile any marketing ideas I have I can apply them to Extra Mile before I test it on anything else. So if I come up with any ideas I ask Julie and she says try it out on Extra Mile. So it's the ideal situation because we can really know what our clients want. And Julie is really supportive as an employer. She encourages me to go out and do things and I've had a few meetings on my own with people and she's trying to get me my own clients to work on and she is really supportive and she's brilliant really.

To finish the interview, I asked Laura what she would like to do after she has completed her apprenticeship. Laura was lucky in that she had a very supportive employer who was an ambassador at the local college. This enabled her to work with college staff to develop new progression routes for Laura and other apprentices in the area:

Julie is an ambassador at Weymouth College. She's trying to introduce a new scheme because after you do a Level 3 apprenticeship there's a massive leap from Level 3 to Level 4. Because Level 4 is like foundation degree, so it's like the GCSE and A level gap. She's trying to get something in between that people can finish their NVQs and then go on to. So like in my case with marketing, I want to go on and do a marketing qualification so I was looking at a Chartered Institute of Marketing certificate. I said I would like to do a certificate with Julie so she said why don't you ask the college? So we asked the college and they are looking into a way to incorporate that after the NVQ, which I think will be a very good idea.

Appendix 4
Useful addresses

Sector Skills Councils

Property, facilities management, housing and cleaning

Asset Skills
2 The Courtyard
28 New North Road
Exeter EX4 4EP
Tel: (0139) 242 3399
Fax: (0139) 242 3373
e-mail: enquiries@assetskills.org
www.assetskills.org

Chemical and pharmaceutical, oil, gas, nuclear, petroleum and polymers

Cogent
Unit 5, Mandarin Court
Centre Park
Warrington
Cheshire WA1 1GG
Tel: (0192) 551 5200
Fax: (0122) 478 7830
e-mail: info@cogent-ssc.com
www.cogent-ssc.com

Construction

Construction Skills
Bircham Newton
King's Lynn
Norfolk PE31 6RH
Tel: (0344) 994 4400
e-mail: call.centre@cskills.org
www.cskills.org

Craft, cultural heritage, design, literature, music, performing and visual arts

Creative and Cultural Skills
Lafone House
The Leathermarket
Weston Street
London SE1 3HN
Tel: (020) 7015 1800
Fax: (020) 7015 1847
e-mail: info@ccskills.org.uk
www.ccskills.org.uk

Business and information technology, including software, internet and web, IT services, telecommunications and business change

e-skills UK
1 Castle Lane
London SW1E 6DR
Tel: (020) 7963 8920
Fax: (020) 7592 9137
e-mail: info@e-skills.com
www.e-skills.com

Gas, power, waste management and water industries

Energy and Utility Skills
Friars Gate Two
1011 Stratford Road
Shirley
Solihull
West Midlands B90 4BN
Tel: (0845) 077 9922
Fax: (0845) 077 9933
e-mail: enquiries@euskills.co.uk
www.euskills.co.uk

Financial services, accountancy and finance

Financial Services Skills Council
51 Gresham Street
London EC2V 7HQ
Tel: (0845) 257 3772
Fax: (0845) 257 3770
e-mail: info@fssc.org.uk
www.fssc.org.uk

Passenger transport

Go Skills
Concorde House
Trinity Park, Solihull
West Midlands B37 7UQ
Tel: (0121) 635 5520
Fax: (0121) 635 5521
e-mail: info@goskills.org
www.goskills.org

Retail motor industries

The Institute of the Motor Industry
Fanshaws
Brickendon
Hertford SG13 8PQ
Tel: (0199) 2511 521
Fax: (0199) 2511 548
e-mail: info@motor.org.uk
www.motor.org.uk

Food and drinks manufacturing and processing

Improve: food and drink sector skills council
Ground Floor, Providence House
2 Innovation Close
Heslington YO10 5ZF
Tel: (0845) 644 0448
Fax: (0845) 644 0449
e-mail: info@improveltd.co.uk
www.improveltd.co.uk

Environment and land-based

Lantra
Lantra House
Stoneleigh Park, near Coventry
Warwickshire CV8 2LG
Tel: (0247) 669 6996
e-mail: connect@lantra.co.uk
www.lantra.co.uk

Community learning, education, FE, HE, libraries, work-based learning and training providers

Lifelong Learning UK
5th Floor, St Andrew's House
18-20 St Andrew Street
London EC4A 3AY
Tel: (0870) 757 7890
e-mail: enquiries@lluk.org
www.lluk.org

Hospitality, leisure, travel and tourism

2nd Floor, Armstrong House
38 Market Square
Uxbridge UB8 1LH
Tel: (0870) 060 2550
e-mail: info@people1st.co.uk
www.people1st.co.uk

Building products, coatings, extractive and mineral processing, furniture, furnishings and interiors, glass and related industries, glazed ceramics, paper and printing and wood industry

Proskills
Centurion Court
85B Milton Park
Abingdon
Oxfordshire OX14 4RY
Tel: (0123) 583 3844
e-mail: info@proskills.co.uk
www.proskills.co.uk

Science, engineering and manufacturing technologies

Semta
14 Upton Road
Watford
Hertfordshire WD18 0JT
Tel: (0845) 643 9001
Fax: (0174) 064 4799
e-mail: customerservices@semta.org.uk
www.semta.org.uk

Sport and recreation, health and fitness, outdoors, playwork and caravanning industry

Skills Active
Castlewood House
77–91 New Oxford Street
London WC1A 1PX
Tel: (020) 7632 2000
Fax: (020) 7632 2001
e-mail: skills@skillsactive.com
www.skillsactive.com

Social care, children, early years and young people's workforces in the UK

Skills for Care and Development
2nd Floor City Exchange
11 Albion Street
Leeds LS1 5ER
Tel: (0113) 390 7667
e-mail: sscinfo@skillsforcareanddevelopment.org.uk
www.skillsforcareanddevelopment.org.uk

TV, film, radio, interactive media, animation, computer games, facilities, photo imaging and publishing

Skillset
21 Caledonian Road
London N1 9GB
Tel: (020) 7713 9800
Fax: (020) 7713 9801
e-mail: info@skillset.org
www.skillset.org

UK health

Skills for Health
2nd Floor, Goldsmiths House
Broad Plain
Bristol BS2 0JP
Tel: (0117) 922 1155
Fax: (0117) 925 1800
e-mail: office@skillsforhealth.org.uk
www.skillsforhealth.org.uk

Policing and law enforcement, youth justice, custodial care, community justice, courts service, prosecution services and forensic science

Skills for Justice
Centre Court
Atlas Way
Sheffield S4 7QQ
Tel: (0114) 231 7375
e-mail: info@skillsforjustice.com
www.skillsforjustice.com

Freight logistics and wholesaling industry

Skills for Logistics
12 Warren Yard
Warren Farm Office Village
Milton Keynes
Buckinghamshire MK12 5NW
Tel: (0190) 831 3360
Fax: (0190) 831 3006
e-mail: info@skillsforlogistics.org
www.skillsforlogistics.org

Retail

Skillsmart Retail
4th Floor
93 Newman Street
London W1T 3EZ
Tel: (020) 7462 5060
Fax: (020) 7462 5061
e-mail: contactus@skillsmartretail.com
www.skillsmartretail.com

Building services engineering

SummitSkills
Vega House, Opal Drive
Fox Milne
Milton Keynes
Buckinghamshire MK15 0DF
Tel: (0190) 830 3960
Fax: (0190) 830 3989
e-mail: enquiries@summitskills.org.uk
www.summitskills.org.uk

Appendix 5
Useful websites

Apprenticeship services

www.apprenticeships.org.uk

This is the website of the National Apprenticeship Service (NAS). On this site you can find out more about all types of apprenticeship in England and use the database to access information about specific apprenticeships. Information is available for apprentices, parents, employers, college staff and advisers.

www.skillsdevelopmentscotland.co.uk

This is the website of Skills Development Scotland (SDS), which is Scotland's skills public body that operates across Scotland as a whole. On this site you can find out more about Modern Apprenticeships and access some interesting case studies.

www.mappit.org.uk

MappIT is an interactive web program that promotes Modern Apprenticeships in Scotland. You can search the apprenticeship database by sector, specialism and locality, or by using the A–Z list. Each entry includes information about the job, training, wage, qualifications and location. Application procedures and employer contact details are also included.

www.delni.gov.uk/apprenticeshipsni

This is the apprenticeship section of the website of the Department for Employment and Learning in Northern Ireland. Visit this site for more information about apprenticeships in Northern Ireland, including information about the different types that are available and interesting case studies from apprentices.

www.nidirect.gov.uk/apprenticeshipsni

This is the apprenticeship section of nidirect, which provides information about government services in Northern Ireland. These pages contain comprehensive information about apprenticeships in Northern Ireland for apprentices and employers.

http://new.careerswales.com/16to19

This is the website of Careers Wales. This section of the site contains information about apprenticeships in Wales and includes a useful Apprenticeship Matching Service.

http://wales.gov.uk

This is the website of the Welsh Assembly Government. Enter 'apprenticeships' into the search box to find information about the various apprenticeship schemes available in Wales.

http://nationalemployerservice.org.uk

This is the website of the National Employer Service, which provides impartial, specialist advice on apprenticeships to employers with more than 5,000 employees. NES employers currently deliver 20 per cent of all England's apprenticeships. If you are a large employer, visit this site for more information about how the service can help you.

Careers advice

www.careers-scotland.org.uk

This is the website of Careers Scotland. More information about Modern Apprenticeships in Scotland can be obtained from this site, along with information about researching a career and applying for jobs. Alternatively, you can obtain more information and advice by telephoning 0845 8 502 502.

www.careerswales.com

This is the website of Careers Wales. More information about apprenticeships in Wales can be obtained from the 16–19 section of this site. Alternatively, you can telephone 0800 100 900 or e-mail the service for advice and guidance about jobs, careers and apprenticeships.

www.careersserviceni.com

This is the website of Careers Service Northern Ireland. Visit this site for information about apprenticeships in Northern Ireland and for general careers advice. There is a useful section for parents on this site.

https://nextstep.direct.gov.uk

This is the website of Next Step, which provides careers advice for adults in England. The website contains information about planning a career, undertaking an apprenticeship and funding further study. You can e-mail an adviser or telephone 0800 100 900 for specific advice and guidance or to arrange a face-to-face meeting.

INDEX